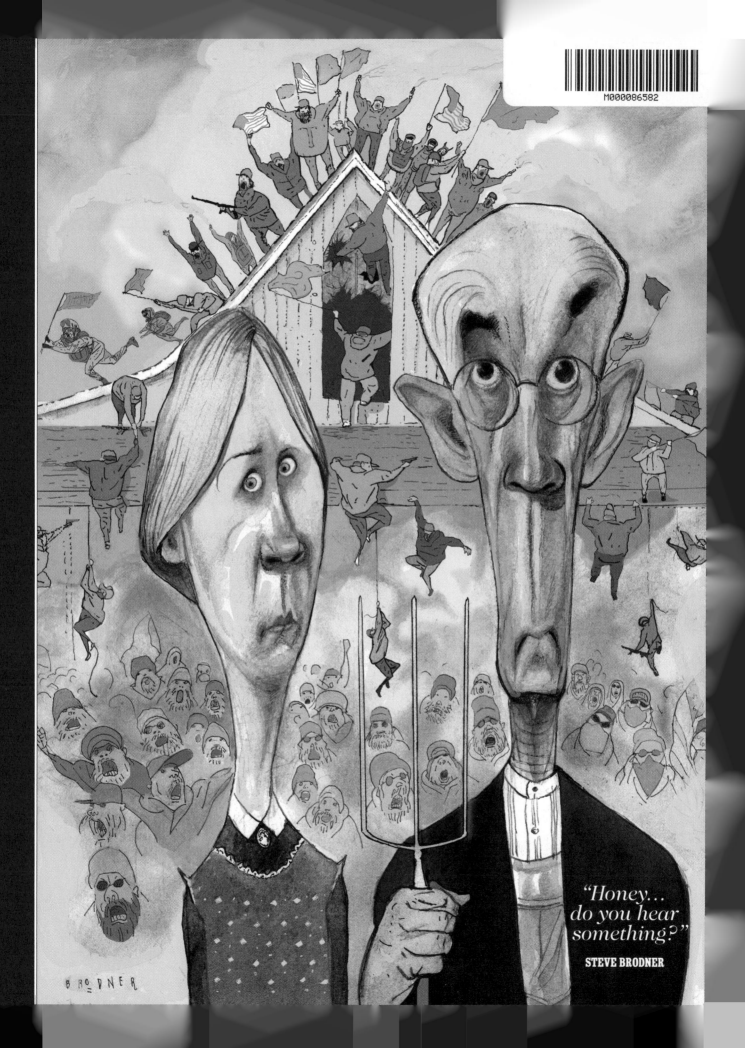

"Honey...
do you hear
something?"

STEVE BRODNER

BY MICHAEL GERBER

CHARACTER STUDY

Know Thyself, and Stay in Thy Lane.

When I was a kid growing up in the bars of St. Louis, the patrons fell into three categories: alcoholics, characters, and adults.

This might surprise you, but the alcoholics were never a problem. I didn't live with them, wasn't related to them, and as long as I didn't believe anything they said, they were harmless. Mom's shift always ended before Happy Hour turned Unhappy.

Then there were the characters. The Central West End was a catchment for a whole state's worth of oddballs, and in Missouri 1975, merely going to college put you in that category. Sometimes just being Black was enough—or blind, or an artist. Or a man who didn't like sports or a woman who did (in other words, gay).

At Llywelyn's, characters were easy to spot: a cape, a ferret, a streak of blue hair, a fake accent, an ability to read Tarot. The only thing you had to watch was stumbling upon their topic, which might be Todd Rundgren or the Kennedy assassination, Maharishi or macrobiotics. The first time I heard about Orgone, it was fascinating; the fifth time, well, you better buy me a Shirley Temple.

A character is a victim of a harmless enthusiasm inflated to gargantuan proportions. They're utterly convinced that they'll change the world in a way that can't possibly happen. Pure-hearted Existentialist heroes. I liked them and they liked me. I got my fortune told a lot.

The bar's adults were, as you might expect, *awful*. The sight of a six-year-old perched on a barstool was enough to make them question everything since

MICHAEL GERBER (@mgerber937) is Editor & Publisher of *The American Bystander*.

women got the vote. When they looked down at me, I felt the judgment go back three generations.

"I don't think this is a very good place for a little boy."

"Why?"

"People are smoking and drinking alcohol. They're using bad language. You could get hurt."

"Lady, have you ever *been* to a playground?"

Even at six, I knew: Never apologize for who you are. Especially to an asshole.

But which was I? Due to genetic luck, alcoholism was out. My parents, anxious for my security, tried to make me into an adult. So did Yale. But I knew what motivated me: Wouldn't It Be Cool If? Wouldn't it be cool if there were meat-flavored gum? Wouldn't it be cool if you could generate electricity through micro-hydraulics in the sidewalk? Wouldn't it be cool if there were a new print humor magazine? This is not someone you want to make CEO of anything. This is someone who works for sixteen years alone in a shack, comes up with tele-portation, and then gets ripped off by Richard Branson. (Richard Branson actually did rip me off one time. I'll tell you about that next issue.)

It's not an easy life, but I think characters are the nicest of the three types—unless they somehow get the opportunity to put their pet scheme into action. Before he was *der Führer*, Hitler was a character in the bars of Vienna. All these tech billionaires, they're characters. too. If you don't believe me, just wait until one of them tries to "fix" global warming with nanoparticles. My lungs hurt already.

Well-meaning people mistaking me for an adult sometimes ask why I don't try to get *Bystander* on the newsstand. "Don't you want millions of people to read it?"

That. Would. Be. Hell. There are 25,000 people, *tops*, sane enough to read this

magazine. Every issue has fifty things I hope never get on Twitter, five of which are in my Publisher's Letter. *Bystander* is a magazine by characters for characters, and while I fully expect us to have our own Playboy Mansion, it will happen in the way wealth traditionally comes to characters: someone's eccentric aunt will choke on a peanut. Or cryptocurrency. That's a business plan, right?

Which brings us to the illustration opposite. In April 1995, I was 25 and living in Seattle's version of the Central West End. Adult or character? My destiny was still uncertain. By day I temped at Microsoft, but every night I sneaked into the 24-hour Kinko's on East John Street to work on a parody of *The New York Review of Books*. I stole hundreds of hours of computer time—blatantly, defiantly, in languid four-hour stretches. The staff, sketching out new tattoos and tending to infected ones, let it slide. I even wheedled a bunch of David Levine spoofs out of an old college buddy. (*Confidential to Todd*: Did I ever pay you?)

I remember carefully Xeroxing all sixteen pages, trying to keep the glued-on pieces from shifting—back in those days, Macs couldn't handle a lot of scans. Then I shipped it off to Robert Silvers, the now-deceased editor of the *NYREV*. This parody clearly killed him.

What happened next? Nothing. What did I think would happen? Unclear—they'd laugh? Take me to lunch? What kind of person creates something this elaborate just for fun?

A *character*, that's who.

The moment that package was mailed, my fate was sealed. I'd be a character—to be worried over and pointed at by the adults, and to the alcoholics a half-inspiration, half-cautionary tale.

Just, I should add, as the Tarot readings had predicted.

B

THE WORK OF A MADMAN: *Incredibly, there are 16 pages after this. Re-reading it today, the parody's cumulative effect is as if Spaceballs-era Mel Brooks had chugged a bottle of NyQuil and fallen asleep watching Sir Kenneth Clark's* **Civilization.**

Garry Wills Versus George F. Will in a Test of Wills

UNAUTHORIZED! UNTAMED! UN-CREDIBLE!

The N*w Y*rk Review

of B**ks

IT'S A PARODY!

$4.95
CAN. $7.00

ASIMOV: THE THINKING MAN'S SEX GOD

(Sorry, Nat!)

BENCHLEY: THE SHARK'S ONLY NATURAL ENEMY

$4.95
CAN. $7.00

The N*w Y*rk Review

of B**ks

UNAUTHORIZED as heck!

Stephen Jay Gould on the Forgotten Science of Mixology

PARODY!

TABLE OF CONTENTS

SHARY FLENNIKEN

The Parts Left Out
of the Trots 'n' Bonnie Book
Page 43

The AMERICAN BYSTANDER

Founded 1981 by Brian McConnachie
#19 • Vol. 5, No. 3 • May 2021

EDITOR & PUBLISHER
Michael Gerber
HEAD WRITER Brian McConnachie
SENIOR EDITOR Alan Goldberg
ORACLE Steve Young
STAFF LIAR P.S. Mueller
INTREPID TRAVELER Mike Reiss
EAGLE EYES Patrick L. Kennedy
251 Adam Chase & Ben Doyle
**AGENTS OF THE SECOND
BYSTANDER INTERNATIONAL**
Eve Alintuck, Melissa Balmain, Roz
Chast, Rick Geary, Sam Gross, *et al.*
MANAGING EDITOR EMERITA
Jennifer Finney Boylan
CONSIGLIERA Kate Powers
COVER BY RON BARRETT

ISSUE CONTRIBUTORS
Elizabeth Albrecht, William Anthony,
Ron Barrett, Lou Beach, Kyle Berlin,
Barry Blitt, George Booth, Steve Brodner, T.Q. Chen, Tom Chitty, Joe Ciardiello, Tyson Cole, Victor Dial, Bryan Duff,
Marques Duggans, Bob Eckstein, Shary
Flenniken, E.R. Flynn, Seth Fried, Lucas
Gardner, Mary Gulino, David Guzman,
Lance Hansen, Calder Holbrook, Sarah
Hutto, Michal Jedinak, Sean Kelly, Ken
Krimstein, Peter Kuper, Todd Lynch,
Libby Marshall, Wes Marfield, Michael
Pershan, Nathan Place, Zachary Pullen,
Sarah Rabinowitz, Denise Reiss, Ellis
Rosen, Laura Savage, Chloe Schneider,
Jim Siergey, Nick Spooner, Mick Stevens,
Pamela Talese, Matthew Thompson, Dalton Vaughn, D. Watson, Kristopher Wood,
Cerise Zelenetz, and Jonathan Zeller.

Lanky Bareikis, Jon Schwarz, Alleen Schultz, Gray & Bernstein, Joe Lopez, Ivanhoe &
Gumenick, Greg & Trish G., Kelsey Hoke.
NAMEPLATES BY Mark Simonson
ISSUE CREATED BY Michael Gerber

.... ◆ ....

OUR BACK PAGES

CARTOONS & ILLUSTRATIONS BY

Ron Barrett, Steve Brodner, Todd Lynch, Shary Flenniken, Sam Gross, Jim Siergey, Nathan Place, Michal Jedinák, Cerise Zelenetz, Ken Krimstein, Tom Chitty, Peter Kuper, Mick Stevens, Joe Ciardiello, Lance Hansen, Marques Duggans, Pamela Talese, Dalton Vaughn, Zachary Pullen, D. Watson, Ellis Rosen, Tyson Cole, William Anthony, Lou Beach, T.Q. Chen, Nick Spooner, Matthew Thompson, E.R. Flynn, Rick Geary, Bob Eckstein.

.... ◆ ....

Sam's Spot

"You're a shoo-in for doggie Heaven."

COVER

RON BARRETT described this drawing to me as "Optimism enters the heart of decay"— and that's how his work always makes me feel. I've wanted to get Ron on our cover since #1, so 2021 is off to a grand beginning.

ACKNOWLEDGMENTS

All material is ©2021 its creators, all rights reserved. Please do not reproduce or distribute any of it without written consent of the creators and *The American Bystander*. The following material has previously appeared, and is reprinted here with permission of the author(s): Shary Flenniken's "Trots and Bonnie" strips first appeared in *The National Lampoon*.

.... ◆ ....

THE AMERICAN BYSTANDER, *Vol. 5, No. 3*, (978-0-578-90967-7). Publishes ~5x/year. ©2021 by Good Cheer LLC. No part of this magazine can be reproduced, in whole or in part, by any means, without the written permission of the Publisher. For this and other queries, email Publisher@americanbystander.org, or write: Michael Gerber, Publisher, *The American Bystander*, 1122 Sixth St., #403, Santa Monica, CA 90403. Single copies can be purchased at www.americanbystander.org/store. **Subscribe at www.patreon.com/bystander.** Other info— probably more than anyone could possibly require—can be found on our website, www. americanbystander.org. Thanks for reading.

EARIOS

THE MARGARET CHO

ICONIC COMEDIAN MARGARET CHO TALKS WITH PEOPLE YOU KNOW, AND PEOPLE YOU SHOULD KNOW.

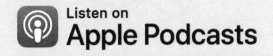

Listen on
Apple Podcasts

Spotify

acast

ACTAEON & ARTEMIS, A GREEK MYTH RENDERED IN THE STYLE OF ERNIE BUSHMILLER

— SIERGEY

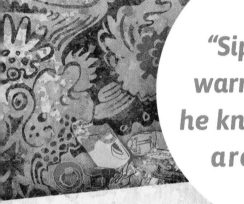

"Sippy tries to warn them all— he knows the bags are trouble!

But underwater, as a straw, his voice is just a bubble."

"An instant classic."
—STEVE BRODNER

"A powerful lesson wrapped in endless charm...beautifully conceived, written and illustrated."
—RON HAUGE

"The Last Straw is a lovely book—a sweet eco-tale rendered in obsessive, passionate detail."
—BARRY BLITT

• • • • • •

Artist **ZOE MATTHIESSEN** takes on the plastic problem in her debut children's book **THE LAST STRAW**

• • • • • •

www.SippyTheLastStraw.com
www.NorthAtlanticBooks.com

SPOTLIGHT

BY NATHAN PLACE

A man with his fingers on the pulse of Stupid America

"THIS IS TAKING FOREVER. LET'S GO BACK INSIDE."

I'M AFRAID OF THE CORONAVIRUS!

NOT REAL. IT'S ALL A CONSPIRACY.

I'M AFRAID OF CLIMATE CHANGE!

DON'T WORRY. TOTAL CONSPIRACY.

I'M AFRAID OF SCHOOL SHOOTINGS!

BIG FAT CONSPIRACY. ALL THOSE KIDS ARE ACTORS.

I'M AFRAID OF CONSPIRACIES!

"DUDE. SIX FEET, PLEASE."

BENEFITS OF WEARING A MASK

1 LEARN HOW BAD YOUR BREATH SMELLS!

2 NOTICE HOW BEAUTIFUL EVERYONE'S EYES ARE!

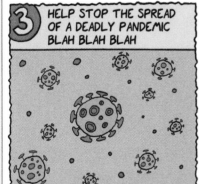

3 HELP STOP THE SPREAD OF A DEADLY PANDEMIC BLAH BLAH BLAH

4 YAWN WITHOUT ANYONE NOTICING!

HRRRR...

"I DREAMT I SHOOK SOMEONE'S HAND."

YOU HAVE **5 MILLION** CORONAVIRUS CASES.

I'M FINE!

YOU HAVE **37,600** GUN DEATHS PER YEAR.

THAT'S NORMAL!

...AND **1,000** DEATHS FROM "INTERACTIONS WITH THE POLICE."

I'M USED TO IT!

ARE YOU SURE YOU'RE OK?

I AM THE GREATEST!!

NATHAN PLACE *is a carbon-based organism that writes and draws things. His comic strip,* Golthar, Terror of the Deep, *is published irregularly on Instagram.*

Gallimaufry

Much of this material comes from our new website,
twofiftyone.net. Check it out!

PROMISE LAND.

Vaccines have arrived! Cue the end of
    the plague!
Though the date when we'll get them,
    for most, is still vague,
We are confident(ish) that—from
    grandmas to tots—
By next summer/fall/winter we'll all
    have our shots.
After that… what carousing! What
    hugging for joy!
From LA to Lake Placid to Ladd,
    Illinois,
We'll be surfing and swimming and
    skiing and sledding
With people we love, unconcerned
    what they're spreading!
We'll join them in restaurants—even
    indoors!
We'll linger in stadiums, loiter in stores!
Then we'll really go wild: we'll pump
    iron at the gym!
We'll go in for a manicure,
    strip wax and trim!
We will mob the museums!
Plus (hardly *de minimis*)
We'll squeeze into
    synagogues, subways and
    cinemas!
Yes, we'll truly be living a
    few months from now—
Assuming, of course, that we
    still recall how.
        —*Melissa Balmain*

INTEGRITY.

Money changes some people,
but not me; I'll never give to
charity.
        —*Jonathan Zeller*

WHALE WATCHING LOG, 4/9/2021.

6:43 a.m.: Going on my first whale
watching expedition today. Very
excited to catch a glimpse of one of
the world's most majestic creatures!
Will be keeping a detailed log of the
adventure.
7:45 a.m.: Setting sail now. Our guide
says conditions are pretty good for a
sighting. Here we go!
9:23 a.m.: Nothing yet
12:01 p.m.: Think we see one! Going
in for a closer look. Exciting!!!
12:10 p.m.: False alarm
1:27 p.m.: Think we see one!
1:30 p.m.: Nevermind
2:55 p.m.: Heading home
        —*Lucas Gardner*

"…and why do you think your sculptures
are so controversial?"

JEDINÁK

ANY DAY.

He said, "Today's not your birthday,"
implying denial of my right
to celebrate for whimsy's sake,
desire presents,
indulge in gifted centricity.

Buckling under his gaze
what else could I do
but acquiesce?

"Aright. I'll pay for the sandwich."
        —*Dylan Brody*

THE FIRST RULE OF COMEDY.

A joke isn't funny if you have to ex-
plain it, so I never explained why I
burned down Todd's house.
        —*Jonathan Zeller*

WHAT 'LL COOL J' STANDS FOR.

Ladies Love Cool James
Ladies Lust For Cool James
Ladies Leap Into Serious Re-
lationship With Cool James
Ladies Live With Cool James
Ladies Lend $820 To Cool
James
Ladies Lag In Their Personal
and Professional Development
Since Focusing So Much Of
Themselves On Cool James
Ladies Lose Track Of Dreams
A Bit For Cool James
Ladies Learn Other Ladies
Love Cool James
Ladies Lecture Cool James

UNFORTUNATELY MISINTERPRETED TATTOO DESIGNS

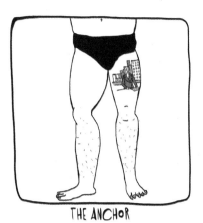

THE BUTTER FLY

THE ANCHOR

THE PIN UP

Ladies Lash Out At Cool James
Ladies Loathe Cool James
Ladies Leave Cool James
Ladies Liberated Without Cool James
Ladies Land On Feet Without Cool James
Ladies Lease New Condo Away From Cool James
Ladies Launch Small Business With No Help From Cool James
Ladies Lavish Themselves Instead Of Cool James
Ladies Lunch With Fellow Ladies That Loved Cool James, Ladies Laugh at Cool James, and Ladies Lampoon Cool James (More like LAME JAMES!)
Ladies Let Time Go By Without Cool James
Ladies Languish In First Holidays Without Cool James
Ladies Lament Cool James
Ladies Learn Cool James Is Now "Working on Himself" James
Ladies Let Themselves Text Cool James
Ladies LOL with Cool James
Ladies Listen to Cool James BUT Ladies Lean On Last Experience With Cool James and Ladies Limit Cool James
Ladies Link Up For Coffee With Cool James
Ladies Let Guard Down Around Cool James
Ladies Look Into The Eyes Of Cool James
Ladies Love Cool James Again

—*Bryan Duff*

HOW TO DEAL WITH MISFORTUNE.

1. Be grateful for what you have.

There's a saying, "I felt bad because I had no shoes but then I saw a man who had no legs." I myself once lost my socks. These were my favorite socks. But then I saw someone who'd lost their whole family in a fire on Christmas and I thought: *Hey, buy new socks!* And it worked!

2. Don't give up.

Suppose someone you love is in an awful accident, and dies—and they were just about to give you a lot of money and didn't put it in writing or tell anyone and now no one believes you. Don't give up—it still can be yours! Just go to the funeral reception and go upstairs and rifle through their drawers and jewelry box till you recoup what's due you.

It's what they would have wanted.

3. Be generous.

What if you come down with a fatal illness yourself? What a welter of thoughts will assail you! But one thing for sure you'll be asking is, *What should I serve when guests drop by?*

First, serve the good scotch you normally hide. Once you're dead, they'll find it anyway—their judgments may be severe.

4. Finally — Seek spirituality.

If you are troubled that bad things

"Hello, IKEA?"

happen to good people, you may despair. Find solace in this spiritual truth: *Bad things happen to bad people, also.*

—*Elizabeth Albrecht*

JOBS THAT WOULD BE TERRIBLE PREMISES FOR PORN.

Funeral Home Director
Methane/Landfill Gas Generation System Technician
CDC Infection Control Specialist
Bereavement Counselor
Roadkill Remover
Asbestos Abatement Technician
Wet Nurse
Elder Abuse Investigator
Beekeeper
Pundit
Traffic Accident Investigator
Gynecological Oncologist
Webmaster
Ethicist

—*Libby Marshal*

A FEW OPTIONS FOR MY TOMBSTONE.

"Don't think of it as me dying. Think of it as one of my infinite selves waking up from a wonderful dream."
Seth Fried
1983-2038
Loving husband,
fell into fireplace

············ ◆ ············

"Now that I've invented time travel, it's time to pants Hitler good."
Seth Fried
1983-1940
Loving husband,
tripped on stolen pants while running from Nazis

············ ◆ ············

"Brb, going to defeat God with logic."
Seth Fried
1983-∞
Loving husband,
choked on Invisalign

············ ◆ ············

"This is very important. Don't write this down. I need a separate funeral for each of my secret families."
Seth Fried
1983-2042
Loving husbands

············ ◆ ············

"Life belongs to the curious."
Seth Fried
1983-2051
Loving husband,
was allowed to see the cockpit on a commercial flight and started touching everything

············ ◆ ············

"You fools. I can't be killed."
Seth Fried
1983-2022
Loving husband,
beaten to death by teenagers while attempting to cheat at laser tag

—*Seth Fried*

HEIST MEETING.

Okay, let's get this heist meeting going. The job is a hard one, some say impossible. But we're going to do it, because you're all the best at what you do.

Razor, our wheel man. He can drive anything on Earth. His mess-up with the Mars Rover does spoil his perfect record, but it's not relevant to this heist.

Snake, our gunman. He has a mystical Glock bestowed on him by a mysterious stranger: it hits anything he aims at with 100 percent accuracy, BUT: every time he uses it, somewhere someone he doesn't know dies. Not the person he's shooting at, a second person. But since Snake's a ruthless murderer and we're all generally amoral, it's not an issue.

Tarzan, our apeman. No one is better at commanding the loyalty of the animals, outside of perhaps the Beastmaster. Oops, sorry T-man. I know I said I wouldn't mention him. Anyway, he's dumb. Who wants ferrets? Apes are better.

Carly Simon, our singer. Nobody does "Nobody Does It Better" better. Admittedly that has limited value, but Carly really came to us and is working pro bono. She can…be a distraction? Sure. Good deal.

And that brings us to me: What do I do? Well, let's just say I'm the best me there is. That's what my mother says

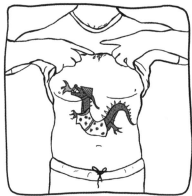

THE CHINESE DRAGON

THE NON HEART

THE SHOOTING STAR

THE PETITE FLOWER

—*Cerise Zelenetz*

anyway. Though dad says my brother of the same name who died before I was born was better. Debatable. I'm alive, he's dead.

Anyway, let's rob this racetrack.
—*Calder Holbrook*

DONALD J. TRUMP'S HISTORY OF HEROIN USE.
1946–2021
No known heroin use
2021–
We just don't know
—*Wes Marfield*

FAMOUS QUOTES FROM HISTORY, IF YOU'D LET THEM FINISH.
"A room without books is like a body without a soul. Or, you might be in the bathroom. Is there a toilet? Yeah, that's the bathroom." *Marcus Tullius Cicero*

"He that is without sin among you, let him cast the first stone. For I have invented a new contraption that I call the 'Dunk Tank.'" *Jesus*

"Do not go where the path may lead, go instead where there is no path and leave a trail. Nope, keep going. That's

it. Just a little further. Oh, I forgot my wallet in the car. I'll be right back... *car speeds off* *Ralph Waldo Emerson*

"Never let the fear of striking out keep you from playing the game. And, just to be clear, I'm talking about prostitutes." *Babe Ruth*

"When you reach the end of your rope, tie a knot in it and hang on. You know what? It would be better if there was a cat hanging from the rope and it just said 'Hang in there.' Make those changes." *Franklin Delano Roosevelt*
—*Kristopher Wood*

FLAPPER HAIKUS.
New me starts today
Oh, how I've let myself go
Fetch my workout pearls

Ethel Gregory
Lost five pounds from Spanish Flu
She's a lucky bitch

Modesty be damned
Chop off my hair and bring me
A looser corset

Harriet, Eunice
Gertrude, Millicent, and Blanche
Are in my girl squad

What in the Sam Hill?
Ethel is hot AND funny?
Pick a lane, Ethel!

Suck it, convention!
I'm going on a solo
Automobile trip

I'm going to wear
My sluttiest knee-length dress
The first time I vote
—*Sarah Rabinowitz*

INTIMATIONS OF GLOBAL WARM-ING—THE LAKE COUNTRY.
Poet, out walking: "Whoa. These daf-fodils are fucked."
—*Elizabeth Albrecht*

THINGS I PASS ON MY WALK WHEN I FORGET MY GLASSES.
1. Shadow monster
2. Cotton candy on a leash
3. A Banksy mural that's way over my head
4. Slender Man
5. Yard full of packing peanuts
6. Pterodactyls
7. Two slabs of tree bark fornicating
8. Dead shadow monster
9. A couple chatting while gently cupping toilet paper tubes in their palms
10. Pool noodles sticking out of the ground
11. The Michelin Man and his lesser known sidekick, Michelin Teenage Boy
12. The harpoon-covered war rig from that opening scene of *Mad Max*
13. A street vendor selling bowling balls at a very reasonable price and golf balls at a very unreasonable price
—*Mary Gulino*

COSTCO OR MY JEWISH GRAND-MOTHER?
1. Up and at 'em at 8 a.m.
2. Will feed you every 10 minutes
3. Unlimited supply of Kleenex
4. TV volume is kept at 41 at all times
5. Crockpot is available upon request
6. Is not always up to date on the latest fashion trends

DISTILLED ELEPHANT

"Hold"
(An interpretive dance)

YOUR CALL IS IMPORTANT TO US, PLEASE CONTINUE TO HOLD...

KUPER

7. Still has wine in a box
8. Nobody under the age of 80 is allowed over before 10 a.m.
9. Peanut butter pretzels are always on the top shelf
10. Five racks of toothpaste can be found by the bathroom
11. Sheet-cakes and cigarettes are un-available
12. Lemon pepper can and will go on edible items
13. Has an eight-foot stack of throw blankets
14. No matter how long you are there, it takes twice as long to leave
15. Doesn't have too many Hannukah decorations, but there's one shelf dedicated entirely to them
16. Endless cups of Kirkland Dark Roast!
Costco: 1, 2, 3, 4, 5, 6, 7, 8, 9, 10, 11, 12, 13, 14, 15, 16
Bubbie: 1, 2, 3, 4, 5, 6, 7, 8, 9, 10, 11, 12, 13, 14, 15, 16

—*Chloe Schneider*

WALT WHITMAN'S FAREWELL TO THE FORMER GUY.

O Captain! my Captain! How dare the snowflakes bitch
That you did anything but steer our ship without a hitch?
What else could you have said to us when krakens were attacking
Besides "Go face them naked! It's a myth that they like snacking!"?
  But the blame, blame, blame
  That the bleeding libtards spew—
  As if you made those krakens gulp
  Us down like barbecue!

D'oh Captain! my Captain! What psychic could have guess'd,
When you were told to walk the plank, it wasn't for the best
To ask a herd of pirates—and some hydras—to come sailing,
And say "We love you" as they torch'd the mast and munch'd the railing?

Then Captain, dear leader,
  What more were you to do
But (sort of) say "chill out, folks" from Your pirate-proof canoe?

My Captain, when the Coast Guard—how's that, sir? Shut my trap?
My "stupid rhymey word group thingy" makes you want a nap?
I'm just a "washed-up creepster type" whose beard leaves you disgusted?

You've heard about my "Lincoln Project" and I can't be trusted?`
  OK! OK! I will admit
  I faked my love for you.
  The krakens and the pirates, though?
  They were fucking true.

—*Melissa Balmain* B

WHERE WERE YOU IN '92?

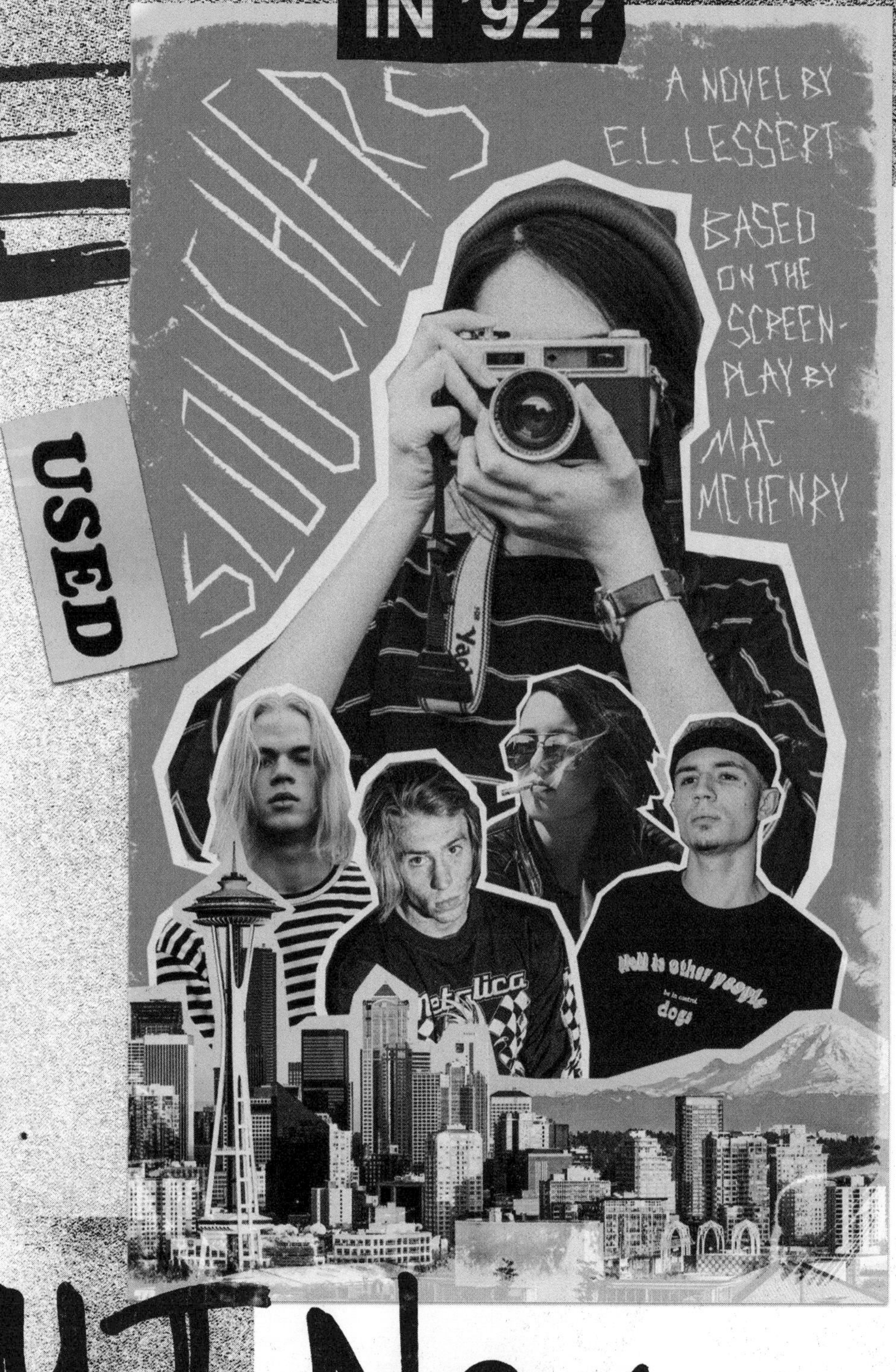

OUT NOW

BY MIKE SACKS

BY SARAH HUTTO

FROM ONE WOMAN TO ANOTHER ABOUT ROBERT PLANT

JOE CIARDIELLO

Hey, you seem new here, and I just wanted to give you a heads-up about Robert Plant. He's going to approach you at some point and say he wants to "give you his love." He means sex. I don't think he's looking for a girlfriend. He pretty much just dates around. Which is fine, I mean, there's nothing wrong with that, but just say that, you know? He should really just say "I want to give you my sex."

And when he talks about wanting to give you every inch of his love, just to shed some light on that, it's basically an inch or two above average. I mean, don't get me wrong—it's all good, and I don't mean to be crass, but that whole "every inch" line is a little misleading. Like, it's nothing to text your sister over, is all I'm saying. I know it looks really intimidating in his jeans, but honestly, I think most of what we're seeing there is a pack of Necco wafers. Also, he's weirdly obsessed with Necco wafers.

When he says "Way, way down inside"? He just means your vag. He's not going to show you some new, magical, secret orifice you didn't know about, or *penetrate your soul*, or some bullshit. It's really just your basic fourteen minutes of missionary.

Also, he's probably going to say he wants to be your backdoor man. I'm not sure he thought that through all the way, but I don't think it means what he thinks it means. I don't know what you're into, but you may have to walk him through that, if you're the adventurous type. He might be using the term in the broader sense, as in some category of relationship, which is kind of comical in this day and age, when so few people live in single-family dwellings anymore that have back doors. Or maybe it's just more of his standard noncommittal B.S., I don't know.

Oh, and he'll keep saying you need "coolin," and honestly, I never figured that one out. Like, if he's asking you to cover up or something because you're turning him on, it's like, "Dude, get a grip." Or maybe it's a temperature thing, but like, let me dictate my own body temperature, you know? *You need coolin'.* Who the hell says that?

One more thing—whatever you do—DO NOT SHAKE FOR HIM. Trust me—just don't. I'll spare you the details, but suffice to say—glass everywhere!

He is fun, though. I'll give him that. If you know what you're getting into, Robert Plant is a whole lotta fun. **B**

SARAH HUTTO (@huttopian) *is a contributor to* **The New Yorker,** **The New York Times,** *and* **McSweeney's.** *She is currently working on finishing a novel she started reading two years ago.*

BY SEAN KELLY

AFTERNOONS WITH FRAU HUBER

In which the author finds that gemutlichkeit *isn't for everyone*

Father Timothy Gallagher, SJ, Prefect of Studies, was concerned about my chronic non-progress in mathematics. "These are the grades of a stupid person," he said, "but you aren't that stupid." (Arithmophobia or numerophobia is a diagnosable and treatable anxiety disorder, but neither my teachers nor I knew that then. We were agreed that the difficulty arose from my reluctance to apply myself.)

Mrs. Huber, Father Gallagher said, was a widow of the parish who lived nearby. Her twin sons had graduated from Xavier some time ago and were now in Munich pursuing advanced degrees in quantum mechanics. She had generously agreed to tutor me in algebra, twice a week, in her home. I was permitted to leave campus and excused from 5 o'clock study hall, but was to be back by 6:30, in time for dinner in the refectory.

The lowest temperature ever recorded in the city of Montreal was –36°F on Tuesday, January 15, 1957, the date of my first math session with Frau Huber.

Mrs. Santa Claus opened the door: a plump, smiling woman wearing rimless specs, her grey hair in a bun, eagerly gesturing for me to enter.

In the front hall I took off my mitts, boots, hat, scarf, and coat. Apparently, Mrs. Claus liked to keep her home cozy and warm. I experienced a temperature swing of nearly 100 degrees.

I could smell newly sharpened pencils. Six of them were lined up on the dining room table, exactly parallel to several pads of yellow, lined foolscap. There were two chairs at the table. Frau Huber took one and gestured for me to sit beside her. With one of the pencils she printed an equation on a page, in letters and numbers so regular they looked typeset. "*Ach so, ach so*, make for me this problem."

I stared at the page. I picked up a pencil. My natural obtuseness kicked in. I shook my head and carefully put the pencil down.

She tried. She was patient. She showed me what to do. Then showed me again. Eventually I wrote down what she had just written as if I had come up with it on my own in a flash of comprehension.

At 6:15, at the door, she handed me a brown paper bag. "*Elisenlebkuchen* from Christmas left over," she said.

On the way back to school, at 36 below, I ate a dozen nutty, sweet, German gingerbread cookies.

Thursday afternoon we were back at the table with the blank yellow pads and dangerously sharp pencils. "*Ach so, ach so*, make for me this problem."

I said, "Thank you for the cookies by the way, they were delicious."

She smiled. "In Bavaria to make *Elisenlebkuchen* we use *Hostien Oblaten*—what you are calling holy communion host."

I gasped, I guess I looked shocked. Was I involved in some kind of Black Mass?

Frau Huber laughed. "Not *oblaten* blessed by a priest, *natürlich*, just ordinary wafer."

She put down her pencil. "I think your trouble with equations is you are hungry from school food, too hungry to concentrate. Perhaps we try an experiment."

Prinzregententorte is a chocolate layer cake. The eight layers, I learned, represent the eight administrative districts of Bavaria. Some minutes later I could confirm, scientifically speaking, that *Prinzregententorte* has no effect whatever on arithmophobia. But as far as I was concerned our experiment had been a smashing success.

Tuesdays and Thursdays thereafter I made almost no progress in algebra but I acquired a deep appreciation of Bavarian cuisine.

While I ate, she took it upon herself to disabuse me of my (she presumed) prejudice against Germans. She herself was

SEAN KELLY *hopes to become a real writer someday. He has nine grand daughters, all of whom are better at algebra than he is.*

from Bayern—"what you say Bavaria"—in the south. "It is Prussians from the North that are mindless criminals, cold like robots. In Bavaria we call all bad people *Saupreussen*. It means 'Prussian lady pigs.' Hitler was a *Saupreussen*."

According to Frau Huber, Bavarians work hard but also play hard. "In the city of Dingolfing the BMW factory makes annually 270,000 of the world's best auto cars but also in München is taking place Oktoberfest, the world's biggest, best party."

Frau Huber served me not any old *wienerschnitzel* but *altbayerisches schnitzel*, and not ordinary sauerkraut but *Bayrisch Kraut*. On one unforgettable occasion, she prepared *Schweinshaxe*, which is roasted pig knuckle with gravy and dumplings, fluffy clouds that she called *Semmel Knoedel*.

Her hometown, she revealed, was Passau, where three rivers meet, one of them the Danube. Her husband, the late Herr Doctor Karl Huber, had been on the faculty of the Ludwig Maximilian University of Munich. He was a theoretical physicist, an associate of Werner Heisenberg. Did I know Doctor Heisenberg?

Karl saw that Nazi persecution of Catholics was only a matter of time, and so in 1935 packed up his wife and twins and came here to Canada. Frau Huber assured me that this miracle was accomplished thanks to the intersession of the *Schwarze Madonna*, a black statue of the Blessed Virgin venerated in a shrine at Altötting.

She assured me that Bavarian beer is the very best, both *hefeweizen* and *ungespundet-hefetrüb*. She never offered me a foaming stein, but now that we had abandoned quadratic equations entirely, we achieved a state of *Gemütlichkeit*, an impossible to translate, exclusively Bavarian condition, she told me, meaning cheerfulness, friendliness, coziness.

LANCE HANSEN

For disciplinary reasons I was grounded for most of that winter, but still permitted to leave the campus for my alleged algebra tutoring sessions with Frau Huber.

Lent had begun in the first week in March, so on this Tuesday I knew better than to expect much in the way of edible treats. When I rang the bell, she answered the door abruptly, almost violently. She was clearly very angry about something. I hoped it wasn't me. I followed her inside. She slapped a newspaper on the table. "Look, look, it starts again."

The headline blared: "Israeli troops leave Egypt. Suez Canal reopens."

"What starts again?" I said. "I'm sorry, I don't understand."

"Zey want another war."

"Who does?"

"Who has started every war?"

She had me there, I had to admit. "Who?"

"Ze *Chews*!"

I had not been previously exposed to this comprehensive explanation of world history. I said, "Wait. Do you mean the Jews started every war? What about, um, say, the American Civil War?"

"ABRAHAM Lincoln," she explained.

I did not personally know any Jews, and though I'd read *The Merchant of Venice*, I had failed to acquire my fair share of traditional lumpen Catholic anti-Semitism. I was sure I had to terminate my gustatory sessions with the Frau, but I had to find a way to do it without hurting her feelings, because I really liked her.

Father Gallagher resolved my moral dilemma. That very Friday, my class had been subjected to a mid-term algebra exam. On Monday I was summoned to the Prefect's office. He sat behind his desk, scowling down at a blue exam book. "Kelly, I've canceled your lessons with Mrs. Huber. It was worth a try," he said sadly, "but it seems you really are that stupid." **B**

BY KYLE BERLIN

PAGING DR. SCHNOZ

Friendly advice from your neighborhood plague doctor

Doctor Schnabel von Rom—'Dr. Schnoz'—is a world-renowned physician, astrologer, and entrail reader. His purgatives and electuaries have been variously embraced at the Courts of Avignon and Castile, and he once gave a course of bloodletting to Pope Clement VI, which cured His Holiness of a yellow humor and much phlegm. When not visiting your local pest house to diagnose the sinful essence of your town, village, or city-state, Dr. Schnoz enjoys a good aperitivo, and scaring the bejeezus out of small children.

Dear Dr. Schnoz,

My good friend Vincenzo, who runs the local *bottega*, refuses to put his flesh-meat on hooks, rather handing it over himself, and will not put out a bowl of vinegar for gold florins, that they might be cleansed of vapor and bad dust. He has even refused to wear a dead toad around his neck, to ward off corrupt air, as mandated by the local College of Physicians. He declares the plague a myth concocted by "quacks like Dr. Schnoz," and says that even if it isn't, a lucky configuration of the heavens will keep his family from harm. How do I convince him that a foul and fatal pestilence is upon the land?—*Sleepless in Siena*

Dear Sleepless in Siena,
As is well known, the first cause of the plague was an unlucky conjunction of the higher planets in Aquarius, namely Jupiter, Saturn, and Uranus. As an astrologer of the school of Ptolemy, and a lifelong votary of Uranus, I can assure you that this conjunction is such a harbinger of mortality, famine, and disease, that it negates any minor configuration as might protect a lying cur like Vincenzo. Have you considered a plague amulet or restorative, such as can be purchased through my network of licensed apothecaries? Now in two new flavors: Green Bile and Black Bile!

Dear Dr. Schnoz,

My brother, Mathias, has lately taken up with a traveling band of flagellants. Every day now, hundreds of them flock to the town square. They strip to the waist, then whip themselves with iron scourges until they bleed upon the cobblestones, while calling out to God to punish the Jews for spreading the plague. At first, we thought a dose of penance might do my brother some good. Mathias has always been a great carouser and lover of ale—and you know how God hates profligacy and carrying-on! But since we got rid of all our Jews in the last pogrom, it's hard not to conclude that the flagellants themselves have brought the plague here. And they don't even wear dead toads around their necks! Half the town is dead, and my daughter now has the mark of the plague upon her. How do I tell Mathias that his new brotherhood is a millenarian cult bent on summoning the Antichrist?—*Worried in Westphalia*

Dear Worried in Westphalia,
Hate to kick a dead toad, but I have to agree with your brother. As you know, Judas himself was born under a bad sign—the fabled Double Conjunction of Uranus, to be exact. Ever since then, the votaries of that magnificent globule have been waiting for the Second Coming, as it were. Now, gazing up at the heavens, it appears that Jupiter and Saturn lie spent, while the Milky Way shines brighter than ever. Coincidence? I think not! As for your daughter, have you tried my new line of all-natural cosmetics, which make even suppurating buboes disappear? Now in two new shades: Deathly Pale and One Foot in the Grave!

Dear Dr. Schnoz,

My fifteen-year-old Oliver refuses to smoke a pipe, despite the protestations of the other boys at Eton, his father, and even the local curate. It's common knowledge that no one who tokes has ever contracted the plague, but Oliver refuses even the meagrest puff. We never thought to have bred such a lily-liver'd boy; his father has threatened to bestow his earldom upon our second son, and even a sound whipping was to no avail. This very morn I felt the nodes around his neck, which seemed to me coiled like tiny serpents. I fear Oliver has the plague—yet even now he refuses, though I roll the tobacco with those same matronly fingers that not long ago he kissed in filial admiration. What's a poor countess to do?—*Lamenting in London*

Dear Lamenting in London,
I feel bound to inform you that the Tobacconist's Guild is such a collection of knaves and ne'er-do-wells as ever walked this mortal sphere. In truth, their 'product' can no more protect you from the plague than smothering yourself in animal suet, or eating lettuce. Even if it did offer some meager sustenance, it is no match for the Double Conjunction of Uranus, that has lately graced the Heavens. As for Oliver, have you considered letting him take the plague waters at the Dr. Schnoz Spa in Baden-Baden? Now offering two new courses: Total Goner and Another One Bites the Dust!

Sincerely,
Dr. Schnoz **B**

has just finished a novel, fulfilling one of his two constitutional obligations as a resident of Brooklyn. He will never, unfortunately, be able to grow a beard.

BY PAMELA TALESE

CAUTION COUTURE

This spring, wow them—from a distance

TALLY HO

Be admired from afar in this fiery frock coat in cavalry twillcloth with a Tattersall lined upper body, black velvet over-collar, and brass buttons paired with thigh-high riding boots. The dynamic contour is achieved by our patented lightweight, flexible tension rods, keeping things breezy for you while keeping others at bay. The fine leather, brass-capped riding crop comes in three or six feet lengths.

OLÉ...AND *OUTTA MY WAY!*

Our ensemble of fitted trousers, jewel-encrusted bolero jacket and super-wide sombrero cordobés with pompom trim is nothing short of striking. It also keeps you safely out of striking distance! With civil society tottering, who doesn't need a little matador *machismo* and a pair of patent leather pumps? This kicky costume is the most perfect balance of masculine and feminine since Almodóvar!

HELLO SAILOR

Ride that Fourth Wave glamorously with our modern hoop skirt! This ultra-flattering frame is covered in our exclusive, vector stopping Invisi-Veil™ in Blue Horizon. An elegant silhouette with marine chic is always current. Add our striped top and coordinating hot pants and it's all hands on *you!* (Metaphorically, of course.)

NUN PLUS ULTRA

Demure *and* daring, this Madonna blue full frock dress with a deep V practically sings, *"Deo volente."* Combining an austere aesthetic with an Eero Saarinen flight of fancy, the multicolor striped, flexible poly/linen cornette can be pulled tightly around the face and shoulders for those eye-of-a-needle occasions. Absolutely divine!

IN THE RUFF

1500 is back! This elegant vector-busting disc is so light you'll barely know it's there—except when you use it to rest your smart phone or tablet. Paired with our form-fitting jumpsuit in Jet/Silver and green gauntlets, you'll look as enchanting as Pierrot and as rocking as Bowie.

SAVING FACE

Sometimes we just don't have the luxury of space. The Narrows, our leaner line for more tailored protection, offers an ensemble for any occasion… Large-collared outerwear in Butter Yellow or Blue Steel. An evening gown—with hood in Mandarin Red—topped with a shoulder piece of curved aluminum strands and whisper fine Invisi-veil™. And when solitude is a *must*, our Military Green boiled wool jacket with deep hood will keep you safely anti-social. Nitrile gloves available in regular and opera lengths.

PAMELA TALESE
(IG: @pamelatalese) is a painter best known for on-site urban & rural landscapes. During 2020, she found watercolor & faux high fashion effective coping mechanisms.

BY DAVID GUZMAN

I HAVE BEEN ACCEPTED BY THE WOLVES

DAY ONE

This morning I arrived in the Northwest Territories on a lone expedition to photograph the elusive Arctic wolf. These beautiful but ferocious animals are notoriously reclusive; to photograph them, I first need to demonstrate to them that my presence here is not a threat.

After setting up camp, I tracked the pack and found them scavenging a recent kill. Upon my approach, their ears perked up; to show I posed no threat, I displayed my naked belly, rubbing it up and down and in a circle, showing them that it was soft and lacked musculature. They looked to each other, then back to my belly, then scurried away. A good start.

Later, I spotted a few wolves near the bank of the river. Knowing they were watching my moves very carefully, I jumped up and hung on a low tree branch, struggling to do even one chin-up. When the branch broke, I cried piteously, showing that I was as helpless as an infant out here in the woods. I laid in the fetal position for some time after that.

In the evening, I refrained from starting a campfire, so the wolves would not be scared. Of course, this meant that I had to eat my food raw, which—luckily—induced vomiting and a high fever, leading the wolves to see me as sickly. *Perfect.*

DAY TWO

While scouting locations, I wandered aimlessly, scratching my head and flipping the map around like an idiot, to give the noble pack perched atop the cliffs the proper impression. Knowing that I couldn't drop the charade, lest the wolves see that I am actually a genius, I "fell" into the river, ruining much of my gear. Getting out of the water, I stripped off my sopping wet clothes, and shivered uncontrollably from the cold. Surely I appeared pathetic—humiliated—but by then the pack had moved on. I had not gained their trust. Yet.

DAYS THREE THROUGH SEVEN

I have refrained from writing, lest the wolves get the impression that I have any type of higher brain function. Growing impatient, this afternoon I attempted to break my own leg. Unnerved by my screams, the pack scattered, so I stopped.

DAYS EIGHT THROUGH ELEVEN

Today, I attacked a beehive. After seeing me get stung dozens of times, one of the wolves seemingly could not bear to watch anymore, and leapt upon the beehive. While I was heartened by this familiarity, his death from multiple bee stings gave the others pause.

Time was wasting; I needed to make a big move. So I ambushed members of the pack while they were marking their territory, knowing that if they urinated on me, I would be at the bottom of their hierarchy. (Plus the fresh warm urine might soothe my stings.) Alas, I was not fast enough and they scampered away. Knowing that one of the males regularly took urination in the grasslands, one evening I emerged from under him, having hidden under the dirt for 72 hours, laying in wait. I expected a howl of domination, but instead the wolf leapt away in terror. I also yelped, as the piss stung. Will my careless vocalization cause the wolves to believe that I am a fierce predator? All may be lost.

DAY TWELVE

Morose, I watched the pack engage in a spirited session of play with the cubs. I intuited that *this* was my chance to play with my gun in front of them, fully cementing in their minds that I am not a danger to them, only to myself. Well, someone must have fired a gun around them before because they totally freaked out. They just…freaked out. And I blew off a finger.

DAY SIXTEEN

After days of depression, I awoke this morning from a drunken stupor (possibly because I ate berries that had fermented, then washed them down with vodka I brought with me) to see five wolves slowly approaching. For one terrible moment, I thought I had been too successful at portraying myself as feeble, and now they would attack *en masse*, tearing me asunder and feasting upon my flesh. I deserved it.

But no. Instead the alpha had gotten ahold of my camera, and pushed it towards me with his snout. The rest of them bowed down, as if begging me to finally photograph them, and end this quest.

They…posed. One after the next. Like so many centerfolds.

I had done it. I had been accepted by the wolves. They no longer saw me as Man, the threat. But as Man, the stung, hungover, nine-fingered fool.

Of course, I needed not pictures of wolves posing, but of wolves in the wild. So I've deleted those photos, and—there must be another beehive around. Or hornets. Or snakes!… **B**

DAVID GUZMAN *has written for the UCB,* **The Onion,** **McSweeney's** *and* **The New Yorker.** *He created the scripted comedy podcast* **Welcome To Wealthy,** *and the audio show* **Advances Of Brain.**

BY MICHAEL PERSHAN

DEPROGRAMMED

Suddenly, the scales fell from my eyes…

Year Zero-Minus-One had been a good year. The mushroom crop was strong, and the majority of our yurts had withstood the harsh New Hampshire winter. Our leader, Dave, had received really encouraging messages from the Eternal Beings orbiting Neptune. "They think our preparations are *outstanding*," he said. "Prepare for The Imminence."

He'd said that before, but I wasn't complaining: the dysentery was almost gone, just as Dave had predicted. And the Anti-Dave had been found in the woods, dead—he'd predicted that, too. And that January, the EB's blessed my wives Dave, Dave, Dave and I with a beautiful baby girl, named "Dave."

It was the middle of the naming ceremony when the Feds raided the compound. We were prepared; Dave had been warning us for years, and we all carried special Neptunian weapons. Well wouldn't you know it, when we fired our lasers, not a single agent melted.

I suddenly realized: we'd all been duped. *The Feds had Neptunian tech too!*

Our only hope was to get to the Teleportation Circle. My wives and I dashed to the yurt and grabbed the kids, which wasn't easy, since the kids spoke only Neptunese and I hadn't paid for lessons yet. And when we got to the pods, things were even worse. From the edge of the woods, we saw the rest of the Exalted standing in the Circle, whispering to the mushrooms and doing the spinning…but nothing was happening. The agents just waited for them to get dizzy, then they'd walk over and slap on the cuffs.

The Feds were laughing too hard to notice us, so we ran for the hills, leaving behind our no worldly possessions.

Just as we got to the Hidden Glade, right near where the Anti-Dave had been found, wouldn't you know it but Dave ran past! This surprised me on so many levels. First, was Dave trying to leave us, his people? Second, if he could run so good, why did he need us to carry him everywhere?

As if to answer, Dave tripped on a root and fell face-first into a pile of snow. Out of his backpack tumbled gold, lots of it—there were my mother's gold bracelets! Dave had told us that Neptunian tech needed gold to work, but there it was.

Suddenly, everything clicked into place: *No wonder our weapons had failed.*

I needed answers; I needed the truth. "Dave, what's really going on? Where are the Eternal Beings? Why didn't our lasers work? Why is all our gold still in your backpack?" My wives looked at me in a new way; I was finally asking the tough questions. "Dave," I barked, "tell me! Are the Eternal Beings trying to test our faith?"

Dave said I was absolutely correct, and that I always had been the smart one. The Eternal Beings had something very special waiting for me when they arrived. I thanked him and he ran off, quicker than before.

That's when my oldest daughter Dave kicked me hard on the shin. "You idiot!" my wife Dave translated. "You goddam fool! Don't you see? Dave is a liar. You are in a cult—we all are. Go catch him before he runs away with Nana's bracelets!" But Dave was already at the top of the hill. He pointed at us and laughed, and called me stupid. Just then, a team of federal agents tased him, cuffed him and dragged him away.

Since that day last winter, I've been trying to rebuild my life. It hasn't been easy. My wives left me. My children all changed their names from "Dave," and now I can't remember which one's which. I've tried to reach out to Dave in prison, but he says his voice won't work unless I give him gold.

Suddenly, it all became clear: *I needed help*. So I joined a support group for ex-cult members.

The group leader was a genius with a goatee named Doc Malcolm. The CIA hired him to create an anti-cult program, but got scared when Doc Malcolm's techniques worked too well. He knows how to free your mind from all limitations. Doc Malcolm told me that I needed to really focus on healing. He ran a center out in Vermont, so I moved into a log cabin with Doc and eight other ex-cult members. I had reached the Ninth Level of Healing and was almost ready for training in Doc's anti-cult methods. It was time to show that I was "in it" for good, so I went to Doc's office to prepare the cash transfer…

You won't guess who showed up just then: Federal agents! I was happy to see them again, and we had a good time catching up.

Once I got myself settled again, I had to admit it: I have a problem. I'm spiritually bereft. I long for meaning that I cannot find within myself. I compulsively seek charismatic leaders to do my thinking for me. I probably wouldn't have figured any of this out if not for Doc Malcolm.

If anybody ever needed a great support group, it was me. That's why I sought you guys out. You're all such great listeners, particularly Brother Clement – your gaze is very intense, but I'm sure you've heard that before! Thank you for lending me a robe, I promise to bring my own next time. I can't wait to connect more deeply with you guys at the compound next week. Who do I make the check out to again?　**B**

MICHAEL PERSHAN

(@mpershan) teaches mathematics to middle and high schoolers in Brooklyn. His favorite number is four.

GREAT DESIGN BOOKS

By Steven Heller

Design School Reader
ISBN: 9781621536901
6" x 9" / 264 pages

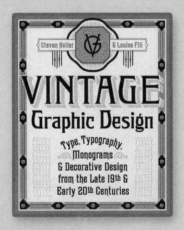

Vintage Graphic Design
ISBN: 9781621537083
8" x 10" / 208 pages

Citizen Designer
ISBN: 9781621536406
6" x 9" / 312 pages

Graphic Design Rants and Raves
ISBN: 9781621535362
7" x 9" / 200 pages

Design Literacy
ISBN: 9781621534044
6" x 9" / 304 pages

Published by Allworth Press in New York City and available
from quality booksellers everywhere.

 Allworth Press

https://www.skyhorsepublishing.com/allworth-press/

Potty training can be a PRICKLY issue.

Laugh out loud with this picture book about a family *attempting* to potty train their new pet porcupine, from *New Yorker* cartoonist Tom Toro. You may almost wet your pants giggling.

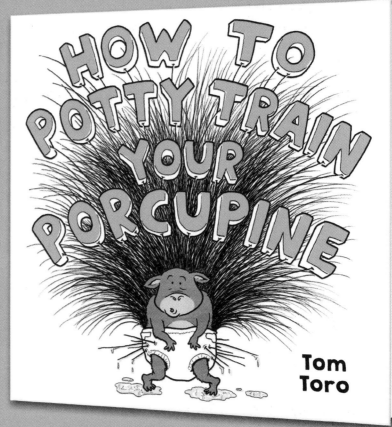

HOW TO POTTY TRAIN YOUR PORCUPINE

Tom Toro

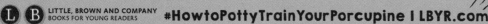

Marrakech

At a dinner party in Marbella (Spain) on New Year's Day 1977, my wife Alix and I were nursing the last remnants of a New Year's Eve hangover. During dinner, our American friend Brewster Palmer IV surprised me when he mentioned that he was an experienced pilot. Brewster had inherited a patrician appearance, a patrician accent, and a patrician name, but alas, no patrician fortune. His financial prospects took a turn for the better however, when he married the heiress to a major pharmaceutical fortune. Sadly, Brewster's wandering eye caused his marriage to come unstuck; but not until after he'd learned to fly his wife's wedding present, a Porsche-like single-engine airplane called a Swift.

When we first met the utterly charming Brewster in Marbella, his wife and the Swift were long gone. But, ever adaptable, he was now living with a lady named Joanna who had had the good fortune to marry—and soon after divorce—a wealthy oil man from Oklahoma. Joanna was enjoying her considerable settlement, alimony, and independence in the sunshine of Marbella, while enriching her sex life with a succession of handsome and muscular lovers.

Also present at our table was my good friend Stanley Cahill, formerly of Southport, Connecticut. I'd first met Stanley years before on an almost-empty TWA flight from Paris to New York. We hadn't known each other, but we were about the same age, and I guess we both looked familiar, so we struck up a conversation. We ended up playing gin rummy for most of the rest of the flight, and by the time we landed we'd become fast friends. Years later he told me I'd made him a million dollars on that flight. (That was a bit of a surprise; I hadn't remembered playing for that kind of money!) It turned out Stanley was promoting some sort of incentive scheme to get Europeans to fill up their tanks at gasoline stations. Those were the days—a very long time ago—when drivers were actually being encouraged to consume gas, and gasoline producers ran promotions to gain market share. Stanley had been in Europe preparing the deal, and was traveling back to meet with Esso in New York to pitch it. At some point he'd turned to me: "Vic, didn't you tell me you're in the car business? Well then, you must know this: how much fuel does a European typically put in the tank when he fills up?" Without giving it much thought I told him it was probably around 35 litres.

Stanley told me later that the first thing he'd done when he'd gotten to New York was to revise his financial model—he'd confused litres with gallons. According to him, had he kept his original projections he would have earned nothing, but thanks to my guesstimation, he'd struck it rich.

But I wander, forgive me. Getting back to January 1, Stanley had recently acquired a new girlfriend, a young and beautiful English lady named Suzie.

So, here we were, enjoying ourselves at dinner with good food and good wine, already feeling a little better, when somehow Morocco came up. After a while, I heard someone—me—suggest that we fly to Marrakech in my recently acquired six-passenger twin-engine Cessna 310 turbo and have lunch at the Mamounia.

"Yes!" said everybody. "Let's go tomorrow!"

As the idea blossomed, Brewster came on even stronger about his experience as a pilot. Joanna snobbishly told us she'd been traveling in private planes all her life, and that it was the only way civilized people travel. Stanley told us he'd wanted to fly for the Navy, but had ended up in the Coast Guard. Suzie didn't say much, but it was clear that wherever Stanley went, she went (smart woman). And my dear Alix was pretty much obliged to come along; anyhow after all the

---

As a result of his many exploits in business and charity, **Vic Dial** *received the Légion d'Honneur—which he hopes to retain, in spite of appearing in* **The Bystander.**

D. WATSON

"Excuse me, do you have a moment to talk about my favorite dinosaur?"

flying we'd done together, she was used to it by now.

I'd never flown to Morocco before and a flight to any new place was an exciting adventure. I had about 600 hours of total flying time, of which 200 or so were in the 310 (call sign N9RV, pronounced "November Nine Romeo Victor"), and I'd earned my instrument rating the year before. I'm a careful pilot, if I do say so myself, and loved to show off my beautiful plane and my flying skills. Here was a perfect opportunity, with a seasoned pilot (Brewster) by my side and a fun group of people in back.

We agreed to go the very next day.

I woke up at the crack of dawn, a bit bleary-eyed I must say, and immediately called the private number reserved for aviation weather at Malaga Airport. I was surprised to hear a woman's voice answer the phone; Franco had only recently died, and women weren't fully "liberated," as yet. I told her I was planning a flight to Marrakech, and asked her about the weather there, the weather en route, and the forecast for the next twelve hours. She said the weather in Morocco would be "fine and sunny." Marrakech? "Beautiful." The forecast

for Malaga? "Nothing to worry about. Everything's marvelous."

Such glowing terms weren't the ones weather briefers typically use: normally they spew out details about cloud cover, winds aloft, temperature, dew point, barometric pressure, significant weather patterns, etc. "Is this really aviation weather?" I asked. "Of course," she answered. "The weather is simply stupendous."

For a moment, I paused; she didn't *sound* Spanish…But I accepted all of this because I expected things to be fine and sunny in Morocco. And my call was a formality anyway, just something a conscientious pilot does, like walking around the plane before takeoff.

I phoned the others to confirm the trip and to get them up and going. We met up at the general aviation terminal at Malaga at ten, as agreed on, and were soon on our way.

The flight to Marrakech takes about two hours, over-flying the romantic, storied cities of Tangiers, Rabat, and Casablanca. And just as forecast, the weather en route was fine.

But then, thirty minutes out of Marrakech, I checked in with Casablanca

Control for the weather and landing conditions at Marrakech Airport.

"Marrakech is fogged in solid," they said. "No planes in or out all morning."

Fogged in? How could this be? And what to do?

I decided to carry on; fog usually burns off as the sun rises and warms the atmosphere. But as we approached Marrakech, it was still foggy. Worse, the sky was filled with airliners from all over Europe, stacked up in a holding pattern. We would be number fifteen to land, if and when the fog lifted.

We joined the holding pattern for a while, but by one o'clock, with no change in sight, I decided to divert to my alternate, Agadir, a 40-minute flight west from Marrakech.

I told my passengers the news; they were not pleased.

"Agadir? Did you say *Ag-a-dir*?" The city had been destroyed in 1966 by a massive earthquake and had been rebuilt virtually from scratch. In the process it had been transformed: what was once a picturesque fishing town was now a thoroughly modern city… with none of the charm of Marrakech. Agadir had a fine beach on the Atlantic, but that was about it. All in all, a poor substitute, but fuel was running low, and we had to land somewhere.

We decided to make the best of it. Our tour of the city confirmed its no-charm reputation, but the guide deposited us at a very nice seaside restaurant for a late lunch. All except the pilot ordered wine, and then more wine, so that by the time we'd finished, my passengers were feeling no pain at all. I even heard: "Agadir's not so bad, even if it's not Marrakech."

In this positive frame of mind, we went to the local souk for some shopping—this, at least, was a relic of Agadir's past. Throwing herself into the spirit of the outing, Alix bought a lovely (and sexy) harem outfit. A fine souvenir from Morocco!

Along with the mandatory purchase of trinkets my passengers also bought several bottles of Moroccan wine for the trip home. "To make the time pass more quickly," they explained.

We took off from Agadir at six, with Brewster once again in the co-pilot seat. I should add here that during the flight down, Brewster's flying ability looked pretty rusty and perhaps even overstated—that was putting it kindly. And considering that he'd been drinking copious amounts of wine at lunch, and had begun sampling the just-purchased local vintages in the taxi on the way to the airport, he'd ruled himself out of any further flying duties. Whatever happened next, I would be on my own.

Fortunately, the flight back to Spain was uneventful, punctuated only by the noisy goings-on of my passengers, by now oblivious to almost everything. Moroccan wine more than makes up for its lack of flavor and finesse with strength.

Darkness comes early in winter, and by the time we reached Tangiers, night had fallen. Thirty minutes out of Malaga, control advised me to expect isolated thunderstorms and light turbulence. Here Brewster could have helped out but he wasn't paying attention. He and Stanley were leading the ladies in a chorus of bawdy songs. I had to ask them to pipe down, because the tower could overhear them when I was on the radio, and I needed to concentrate on what I was doing. There was indeed a lot of turbulence, and the plane bounced around a bit, but I seemed to be the only one who noticed, or cared.

To complicate things a little more, there was other traffic, and I had to hold over the Malaga NDB (non-directional beacon); this is one of the most difficult manoeuvres in flying, difficult to do well even in good conditions, and these were definitely not good. Ignoring the songs, I managed the whole process successfully. It had been a fun trip, and as always I was glad to have brought my passengers safely home. We jumped into our cars and headed back to Marbella.

At home Alix and I changed clothes and got ready for dinner; dinner is late in Spain. Alix put on her brand new harem outfit, and off we went.

There were thirty people at dinner, seated at three tables. We regaled our table with a lurid, highly fanciful version of our day trip to Morocco. But imagine my surprise when during a lull in the conversation, I overheard a lady at the next table describing the amazing phone call she'd had early that morning from a crazed Englishman asking about the weather in Marrakech.

"It was obviously a prank," she said, "so I just made up the first thing that came into my mind." Only after she'd hung up had it occurred to her that the caller might have dialed a wrong number, and might have actually believed her.

"Then I began to worry, really worry," she said. "What if something terrible happened to him? It would be my fault!"

As I listened in, my first thought was: "Serves her right! She should've never pretended to be a weather briefer in the first place—let her stew!" But then my heart softened; I'd better go over there, introduce myself, and reassure her that no harm had been done.

Just as I was rising out of my chair in a gentlemanly fashion, I heard her male dinner partner say in a loud voice: "Ridiculous! No one could possibly be that stupid."

I decided to stay where I was.

After dinner, we all danced. Alix's harem outfit drew a lot of attention, most notably from my weather-woman's partner. "That outfit is sensational," he said. "How much do you want for it?"

"A good deal more than you'd want to pay," I said, "considering you'd have to fly to Agadir by way of Marrakech. But don't worry—'the weather is simply stupendous.'"

Epilogue

Soon after, Joanna concluded that propeller planes were too small and too slow; she upgraded to jets. After several more years and as many exhausted lovers, she married an elderly count, and is now a countess.

Brewster told everybody about how he'd "flown to Marrakech and Agadir for the day," forgetting to mention that there had been another pilot in the plane. He moved back to New York some years later; the last time I saw him was when we met up at Amaranth for dinner, and found ourselves the only males at a bachelorette party (now that was fun).

Stanley and Suzie spent most of the trip sitting in the back making out. They eventually married, but Stanley passed away far too soon. I never did get my share of the million I helped him make.

A few years later, the weather forecaster, a beautiful Swedish lady named Anina—I swear I didn't know her at the time—married my great friend Luis Cuevas, a frequent paddle tennis partner. Whenever I see her she calls me "Victor the pilot" and tells me she's never forgotten that early morning phone call.

Neither have I.   B

"This isn't what it looks like. I'm shopping."

Animals' Inhumanity to Man

WILLIAM ANTHONY

*Works by New York-based painter **William Anthony** have been collected in over 30 museums worldwide. A visitor to one of his shows once said, "Oh, that must be the work of a retarded person."*

THE ORIGIN OF THE EASTER HARE

------- ◆ -------

It's 1643 in the Kingdom of Prussia, as an otherworldly finger of lightning arcs towards the city of Naumburg.

Local denizens run for shelter, but an ill-fated few are caught short. Three animals, as if chosen by Zeus, are ignited and momentarily fused.

These creatures perish, but not in vain. The hen is egg-laden and her offspring survives.

A FORTUITOUS MELDING

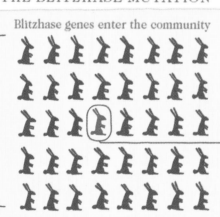

electrical spams

whistling

cock-a-doodle-done

fried bacon

shaken tail feathers

leg

alive

wattle

THE BLITZHASE MUTATION

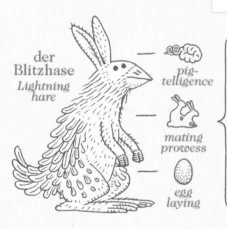

der Blitzhase
Lightning hare

pig-telligence

mating prowess

egg laying

Blitzhase genes enter the community

A small number of each generation present heightened smarts and retain the ability to resolve an egg.*

growth mindset

*sweet egg-like pellet

BIRTH OF A LEGEND

The Spring feed

an ushering

curiosity

discovery

reverence beyond measure

Human veneration of the Lightning Hare ensured its survival, but their keen desire for oval treasures was at odds with its timid nature. Hence, to stymie these inquisitions, the moonlight ritual of pre-emptive deliveries was born.

Aided by rapidly evolving intelligence, and technological advances, der Blitzhase has remained unseen for hundreds of years -- though few in that time have failed to delight in its expulsions.

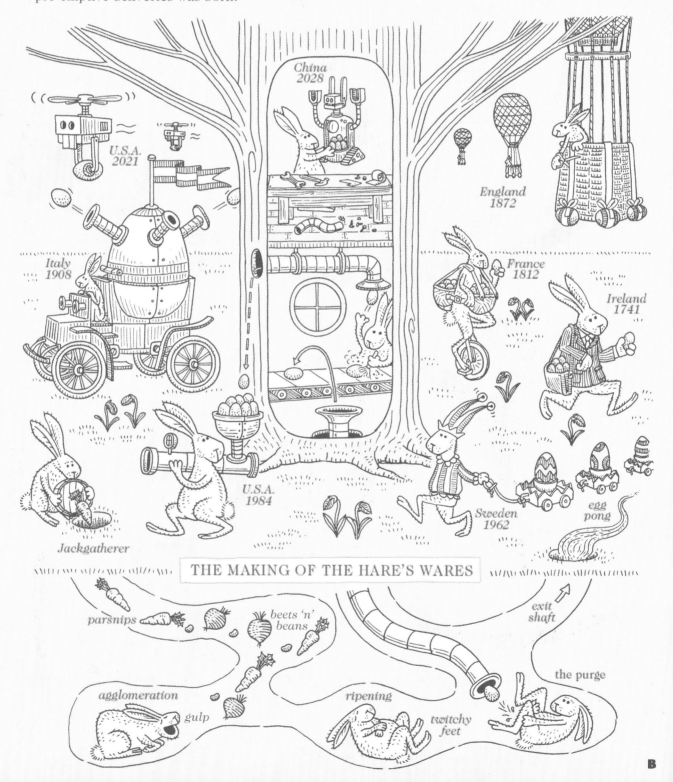

China 2028

U.S.A. 2021

England 1872

Italy 1908

France 1812

Ireland 1741

U.S.A. 1984

Jackgatherer

Sweden 1962

egg pong

THE MAKING OF THE HARE'S WARES

parsnips

beets 'n' beans

exit shaft

agglomeration

gulp

ripening

twitchy feet

the purge

B

A Spirited New Podcast

With the Coolest Names in Cartooning from

WEEKLY HUMORIST

The

Cartoon Pad

With Hosts Bob Eckstein & Michael Shaw

Shaken & Stirred
Bi-Weekly

Outtakes

NY Review Comics has published a collection of "Trots and Bonnie," Shary Flenniken's beloved strip from **The National Lampoon.** *When Shary shared the good news, I asked her to set aside a few strips that didn't make the book; "TnB" was such a product of its era, I wanted to reprint a few with Shary's comments, to show how times have changed…and the artist, too.—M.G.*

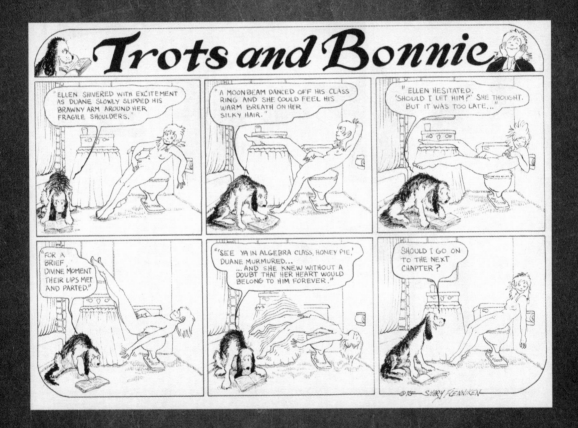

1975

"BONNIE'S PRIVATE MOMENT"

The 1970s were so brazen. Looking back, I feel guilty about exploiting my cute comic character like this. At the time, I thought that I was educating *The Lampoon's* 18-to-25-year-old male demographic about what female sexuality could be like. After 1977, when VHS tapes invaded America, boys too young to get into sleazy art theaters could get their sex education from their father's private video collection. But in 1975 when I wrote this strip, I was doing *Lampoon* readers a favor by showing them something that even *Playboy* did not—that girls too, locked themselves in the bathroom and beat off.

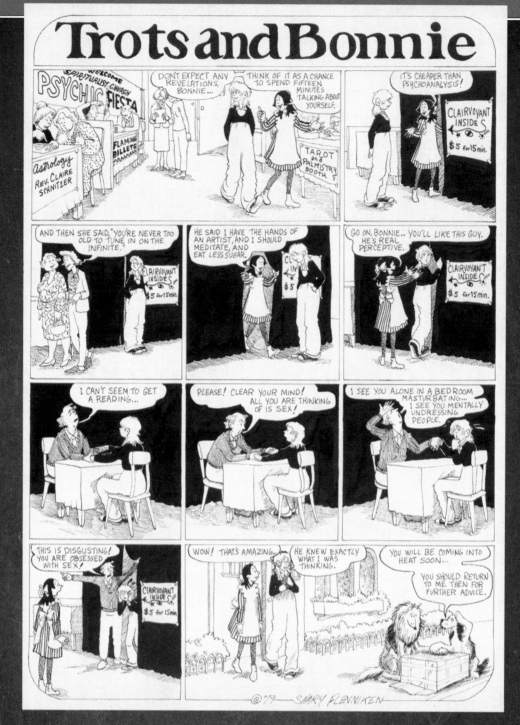

1978

"PSYCHIC FAIR"

I wrote this strip when I was living in St. Petersburg, Florida, in 1978. There wasn't much to do there except get drunk or go to the beach or both. But Florida is where the traveling carnivals like to go in winter, and they can be a lot weirder than a simple Psychic Fair. At a winter carnival for example, when you pay to "See Gator Woman!" you will see a guy wearing a blonde wig. He is standing under the stage with just his head poking up through a hole in the floor. Attached to his neck is the headless carcass of a stuffed alligator. He *is* scary though, because he gets very angry when you laugh at him.

Paying a psychic to tell you about your future is even more unnerving. Imagine someone invading your brain in order to learn more about you than you yourself know. You've read about it in many novels, but it takes courage to pursue it in real life.

However, I was still in my twenties and presumably invulnerable, so all systems go.

In this comic strip, Bonnie endures my worst nightmare. In real life, it's a letdown to realize how long you have to wait to find out if the predictions come true.

1979
"BONNIE'S DEPRESSION"

There's something about riding the subway in New York that made me feel small. Minuscule, like a grain of sand on an infinitely polluted beach. You really notice the vastness of human life on earth when you are crammed on a subway car.

Naturally, those were times when I would contemplate the huge volume of pee that everyone in that subway car could produce and the square feet of toilet paper they would use.

If you think too much about bodily functions en masse, it quickly leads to wondering why we are all here. At least it did for me when I was pushing thirty and new to the third largest city in the world.

Here's a hint. If you start feeling that far down, you probably need to take a nap.

In my case, I had a deadline to meet so I wrote this strip that expressed exactly what I felt—but with a hopeful ending.

1979

"PARROT TALK"

I am obsessed with consumerism. I live on the cheerful end of it, collecting electronic devices with the technological half-life of a flea and kitchen gadgets I seldom use. My basement pantry doubles as a fully equipped bomb shelter. Extreme anxiety causes me to purchase shoes and junk jewelry. I own at least triple the number of things that I need.

Having said this, I envy the simple life. Tiny houses. Unassigned interior space. A very short to-do list. Limited options. For me, the best part of a vacation is being able to live out of a suitcase.

Looking back at my comic strips, I can see that many represent a vehement anti-consumerism crusade. Some part of me resents the corporate manipulation of cute TV commercials and catchy jingles. How dare they occupy so much acreage in my brain? In this strip at least, I could use Trots as an attack dog to annihilate a peddler of corporate capitalism.

1980

"PEPSI'S POETRY"

You write poetry, right? Everybody should. It is the only art form where you are certain to be free of any corrupting financial incentive.

In Trots and Bonnie World, song lyrics and poems are perfect vehicles for my personal diatribes. Pepsi echoes my resentment of male fantasies that include garter belts and crotchless panties. I mean, what good are panties that don't catch the drips?

In the end, like so many artists who dare to speak the truth, Pepsi is attacked by the very people she is trying to represent.

1984

"ALL-MALE BEAUTY CONTEST"

If you examine my comic oeuvre, you may notice that for me, gender equality means equal sexual objectification of men. I have worked hard to do my part to level the playing field. Unfortunately, even now we do not see enough sexy male flesh. Unless you count those thin bike tights that male cyclists wear. And plumbers.

And gay men—they understand male sexiness.

In 1984, when I wrote this comic strip, I was living on 11th Street in Greenwich Village.

We couldn't think about sex without being conscious of AIDS. Pepsi's awarding the prize to the guy in the giant condom suit wouldn't have made sense to the Funny Pages readers even a year before this page appeared. AIDS soon changed forever the way we look at sex and relationships. Like mask-wearing today, using condoms reflected a desire to protect others.

1989
"GRAFFITI ART"

I think it took Vaughn Bode's luscious cartoon art style to make everyone realize that graffiti is public art. Decades after his death, energetic kids with spray cans emulate his characters and lettering style on the walls of buildings and the sides of freight cars all over the world.

Other great artists have made their careers by taking advantage of graffiti's free exposure in public places.

In 1984, when I wrote this strip, Jean-Michel Basquiat and Keith Haring were alive and thriving. Of course, Pepsi was driven to emulate them.

Pepsi understands the basic principle of art—your name is what you want people to remember.

1989

"PEPSI'S PRAYER"

I'm sorry. I deeply apologize for any racist connotation of this comic page. In 1989, when I wrote it, there was little question—at least in my head—that black men had little to none of the kind of (political) power that Pepsi craves. That's the punchline.

To this day, I cannot imagine any woman who wouldn't rather have been born a man. Peeing and periods—it's that simple.

I always knew my parents wanted me to be a boy. After a succession of deceased siblings, I was my forty-year old mother's last chance and she rolled snake eyes. My father couldn't help but long for a son to follow in his footsteps to the Naval Academy. I absorbed my parents' unspoken messaging when they gave me toy guns and a Davy Crockett outfit complete with fringed jacket and a plastic coonskin cap. I gleefully accepted the challenges of boyhood until that critical age when the dreaded characteristics of female puberty intruded on my body. It's no coincidence that Bonnie has been frozen at age thirteen, continually attempting to adjust to the stunning onset of adolescence.

Fauxnana

I am a call girl. You'd think after coming to it late and doing it for most of a decade, I'd graduate to "call woman"—but such are the vagaries of the business.

And it's a good business, once you get your branding and advertising dialed in. Anybody can have sex; it's the marketing that makes you, and what can I say, I'm gifted.

I love my job. I earn a good living, pay my taxes, and meet a lot of interesting people. Doctors, lawyers—politicians, naturally—guys in the C-suite…Men with abundant lives; ritzy apartments and summer houses, wives and girlfriends. Good sex lives—but things they'd never dream of asking the Mrs. to do.

One of my most interesting clients was a man I'll call "Will." He reached out to me one summer evening, asking about an extended private date early that fall. "I'm flying out of your city to visit my son. I'd love to see you the night before."

Sounds like a plan, Will. He was respectful during our brief emails and met all my requirements for screening and safety. I booked the date and forgot all about him until the evening of.

Dressed in a red cocktail dress, I met Will at his swanky hotel suite. He was a very dashing man in his late sixties or early seventies, a John Forsythe type. He wore a button-down shirt, blazer, and trousers. Perfectly coiffed white hair. His teeth were straight, white, and all his own. Good for him.

I discreetly tucked the envelope of cash in my clutch and stepped into the bathroom to count it while Will poured up a glass of something bubbly. The business portion of the evening concluded, I walked back into the room thinking this would be a walk in the park. Will was older, certain to finish quickly, and then we'd fill the rest of the four hours chatting politics, art, classic film. Easy-peasy.

Or so I thought.

Although I have pretty good kink-sense (I can tell if a man likes being pegged by how he walks through the produce section of Whole Foods), I didn't see Will's fetish coming. And I've never experienced anything like it before or since.

Polite chat continued. I made my move by sliding my hand up his thigh and biting my lip while giving him "the eyes."™ Will read my signals loud and clear, and before long we were mostly naked on the king bed.

Will was a considerate man. He had brought his own condoms and lubricant for our date. As I made my way down Will's liver-spotted body, he reached for the large bottle of lube.

"Here, use this," he muttered.

The bottle itself was a bit dusty—and my god, was it big. It had a bright orange price sticker on it: $4.99, and was the kind of thing you'd find at a seedy truck stop sex shop. I popped the top and was immediately hit with the scent of factory banana. Flavored lube isn't a favorite of mine at any time, but *banana*? This would require professionalism.

I squirted a quarter-sized dollop in my palm and greased Will's penis. "Suck it?" he pleaded.

Amazingly, the lube's taste was worse than the smell. Sickening sweet and…vaguely metallic? This was going to be rough.

"More," he moaned.

I picked up the pace.

"No, not faster. *More*."

I smiled sweetly. "More what, love?"

"More lube."

Well, okay, then, sure. I squeezed another healthy dollop onto his cock.

"More," he sighed.

Another healthy squirt with a bonus bottle fart at the end. Will was thoroughly aroused. "Hand it to me."

I passed him the bottle. Will shook the bottle once, hard, and drew a figure-eight on his chest with it. His hands went straight to work, sliding the lube all over his hairless torso.

"Your mouth, please," he begged.

But the fauxnana, my brain screamed. "Of course, Will," I purred in my best high-end call girl voice. "My mouth."

I steeled myself and went back to the blow job. "Laura," I said to myself, "you must not puke on this kind, perverted old man."

The taste. The smell. The stickiness. This hellish goo defeated the whole purpose of lube; the more you used, the tackier everything got. They'll have to burn these sheets, I thought.

I glanced up at Will; he was licking his lips, bottle in hand. Moaning from the back of his throat, he dolloped two walnut-sized globs, one on each of his flat nipples. "More lube," he breathed, and passed the bottle.

············ ◆ ············

Laura Savage (@thatlaurasavage) is a writer, consultant and dominatrix based in the Northeast. She is working on a memoir and a novel.

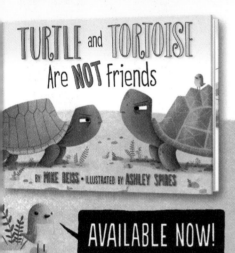

What the hell, I thought. More lube it is then. This time I really went for it, squirting wildly from belly button to mid-thigh.

"Dear god yes, this is so hot," Will said with a grimace of pleasure.

If you say so, my guy. "So hot, and sticky," I purred.

"Keep talking like that."

I did and it wasn't too long before Will finished. Both my client and his econo-sized bottle of lube were thoroughly empty.

We had some pillow talk, my body pressed up against Will's. The smell of banana-with-notes-of-burnt-plastic wafting through the room. Would they have to burn the drapes, too? It was a possibility. When I left the bed to freshen up, our bodies made a sound, a wettish sort of squeak, like sweaty ass cheeks when you stand up from a leather couch in August.

Washing was useless; this fauxnana devil actually repelled water. It pilled on my skin in greyish balls. It had even gotten into my hair, which was stuck to-gether in a crusty mess. Gross. I threw on my lingerie and dress and resigned myself to my fate; I would walk out of the Four Seasons in a cloud of fauxnana with lubricant tangled in my hair. It took all the dignity, and nose-deafness, I could manage.

I could smell fauxnana in the car on the way home, and although I took two showers before bed, I could still feel it under my fingernails and taste it in the back of my throat the next morning.

Will emailed me the next week. He'd had a great time. The best time ever in fact. He'd love to see me again the next time he was in town.

"I'll look forward to it, lover." A lie, but customer service and everything.

A few weeks later, I had a *menage a trois* with another working girl in my city. After the client left, we lingered, smoked a bowl, and I told her the story of Will and his lube. We laughed.

Will emailed me again four months later. "Back in your city next month. Round two."

Christ in heaven. "Absolutely," I replied.

I was ready this time. I got my head-space right and didn't bother blowing out my hair. I knew I would throw my lingerie away after the appointment, as I did last time. Because—news flash—that shit doesn't wash out.

Will arrived at my hotel this time and brought me a gorgeous potted orchid. Chocolates. Edible panties. And there in the gift bag was another ketchup bottle-sized container of Satan.

He winked at me. "We had such a dirty time last time. I can't wait to do it again."

"Inside, he's just a scared little boy who hates people with different ethnic backgrounds."

TOUGH LOVE TRIANGLE

LOSE THE HAT

YOU NEED TO BATHE

NOBODY LIKES YOU

CNiHy

"Mmmm, neither can I," I grinned. "Let's get sticky."

Round two went much like round one. I went in full force, facing the unpleasantness head-on. I squirted lube everywhere, and even gave Will a little show by sliming up my tits. He liked that a hell of a lot.

Never got around to the edible underwear, but that's fine. We finished up sticky and sweet, pressed together with the lube gooped up between us.

I took three showers after he left and threw out my clothes. It almost eradicated the smell. I could live with this.

I saw Will three more times. Each visit was the same. Now that I was prepared, I looked forward to his messy play, in a detached, curious way. As with most fetish clients, I was happy to provide a safe, accepting space for this guy to get his freak on.

A few weeks after our last date, my work phone rang. It was the call girl I had the threesome with months ago.

"What was your lube guy's name?"

"Will," I said. "Why?"

"I think I just saw him."

"Holy shit. Are you serious?" I laughed. "What was that like?"

"Sticky. Strange. I can still smell it even after a shower."

"Yeah, banana lube'll do that to you."

"Banana? It was cherry."

Now I was fascinated. Does this rascal have a different fruit for every girl? I must know.

I didn't have to wait long. A month later Will emailed me.

"Hello Banana Girl." (I was right. The glorious weirdo.) "Back in town in six weeks. Want to play?"

"Will, I wouldn't miss it for the world."

Things can get hectic in my job, so Will's appointment snuck up on me. I was on my way home from a long lunch that involved watching French porn while a VP of Sales and Marketing jerked off on my feet, when my iCal pinged. I sent Will a quick text: "Looking forward to tonight, Banana Boy."

Moments later, I received a text. "Who is this? Are you trying to reach Will?"

Uh-oh. Then, five minutes later:

"This is Will's wife. I'm sorry to say he passed away three weeks ago."

"Wrong number, I'm so sorry." And I was.

My phone indicated that she was typing a message, but I blocked the number. I don't text with wives.

Why was I Fauxnana and my colleague Cherry? I never got the answer, but if there's a heaven, I hope Will's there right now. Where the lube bottles are truck stop cheap and large. Will's bliss. Endless flavors of factory fruit and a girl for each flavor. Go gentle into that good night, Banana Boy. **B**

Is That You, Tebow?

A fancy restaurant in New Orleans. The world's worst chef. What could possibly go wrong?

Before working as a line cook, my idea of a homemade meal was any one in which I pressed the microwave button myself. I would say that I was a bad cook, but that would be an insult to bad cooks. Because even the worst cooks still, you know, cook. I was a non-cook. An anti-chef. A sucking black hole of culinary ignorance, draining the light from anyone who tried to show me how.

Naturally, I took this as a hint that I would be really great at it.

Not to get all possessive, but this is sort of my thing. One time, on a ski trip in college, I waited until I was on the chairlift to admit I had no earthly idea how to ski. Four blue runs, three hours, two sprained wrists, and one broken thumb later, I made it back to the resort—all without help from the fake news Ski Patrol.

So you could say I succeeded.

You won't, of course, because you're not an idiot. But you could. After all, I had done the dumbest, most humiliating thing imaginable. Where else was there to go but—okay, in this case, down.

You get the idea.

Anyway, at the time of this culinary epiphany, it was 2011, and I was living in New Orleans. Six years after Hurricane Katrina, abandoned buildings and homes were still commonplace across the city, a visible reminder of the tens of thousands who had left and never returned.

Even so, no chef was desperate enough to hire a 22-year-old journalism major who thought "haute cuisine" was a fancy way of saying "warm food."

Even so, no chef was desperate enough to hire the bozo who waited until he was on the chairlift to admit he could not ski.

Right?

Wrong. Chefs love that shit. They want someone who has an incredibly high tolerance for pain and humiliation. They want someone with no preconceived notion about how things should or should not be done. They want to break you down, so they can build you back up. If he hadn't been a drill sergeant, R. Lee Ermey would have been a spectacular *sous chef*.

Just think of the things he could do with a jelly doughnut.

So I applied for a job at Coquette, one of the first fine dining restaurants to open after the storm. Why the chef hired me, I'm still not sure. Some possibilities:

→ I was an easy hazing target.
→ I was an easy hazing target.
→ I was an easy hazing target.

On my first day, in keeping with the *Full Metal Jacket* vibe, my old identity was discarded, and I was given a new one. Here's what happened.

I was sent to the walk-in to get "mirepoix." I had no idea what it was. I had no idea how to spell it, even. They knew that, obviously.

When I finally came back—carrots, onions, and celery in hand—the entire kitchen was locked in a huddle. I heard laughter, and whispers. It sounded like: "He does! He does!" The chef was passing his phone around. The whispers continued, lusty and a little unhinged. "He does! he does!"

When the chef finally realized I was standing there, he turned to me. On his phone was a photo of Tim Tebow, who was still in the NFL at the time, and something of a league-wide joke.

☞

Kyle Berlin *makes a killer shrimp and grits, and a very respectable chicken and waffles. He can cube carrots in his sleep.*

Now just so we're clear, I look like America's most famous celibate as much as any other tall white guy.

But that didn't deter our dishwasher, whose name, I swear, was Leopard. Leopard was an ex-con with gold caps on his teeth and a thick New Orleans accent. "That motherfucker looks *just* like him!" Leopard crowed. The chants grew louder. "He does! He does! *He does!*"

From that day forward, I was "Tebow." It was better than "Gomer Pyle," I guess.

My drill sergeant was Chico, which was his real name, just like "Private Joker" and "Leopard" are real names. Chico was a balding, middle-aged Irishman. He was a recovering meth addict, and a proud alcoholic. He also had a penchant for "accidentally" groping us as he moved down the line, which was kind of a joke, but also not.

He was, in other words, a fantastic cook.

In the middle of service, Chico could leave his station, walk down the street to our local Irish pub, take a shot of Jameson, smoke a cigarette, come back to his station, smoke another cigarette, fondle some male chef booty, and still put up plates that looked and tasted far better than anything I could manage, in a fraction of the time.

"Dirty station, dirty mind," were Chico's watchwords, which he would always follow with a disgusting joke. Usually about being gay. Which he definitely wasn't. Which none of us were.

Definitely.

As for the rest of the kitchen—admittedly, it was a motley crew.

There was Richard, the giant from Virginia with the Mugatu hair and knockwurst fingers. Like a dancing bear, we kept him chained to the grill, because he was too big to fit on the line.

There was Gonzalo, who sent a large portion of his check home every month to his native Honduras, in order to support his beloved cock-fighting ring.

There were the Ball brothers, Michael and Chris, who were New Orleans famous for their long, dark hair, and matching "WOMB MATE" tattoos, inked across the knuckles.

(Which was not even close to their dumbest tattoo. The prize, I think, goes to Michael: One pig taking another from behind, with the caption "MAKIN' BACON.")

And then there were the many courageous female cooks we worked alongside, who will have to appear in the movie version of this story, because we never hired them in real life.

In fairness, you can see why they might have been hesitant to apply.

Also, the groping thing.

Anyway.

"Tebow, you cut chives like old people fuck. Slowly, and with no discernible skill."

"Tebow, tonight you will sleep with your knife. You will give your knife a girl's name—Kyle, perhaps."

"Tebow, are you really saving it for marriage? That is some sad shit. But not nearly as sad as this droopy-ass excuse for a salad."

Those are the nicest things that were said to me.

In this way, a year went by. But I survived. I improved. Gradually, I unfucked myself. I became comfortable handling "Kyle," and a sauté pan. I learned how to blanch, and braise, and even *brunoise*. (Look it up.) When I was panicked, or stressed out, I no longer caromed around the kitchen like a "drunken Gumby," or an "epileptic Mr. Bean," or "the tragically mangled love child of Mr. Magoo and a spastic giraffe."

Did I mention Chico loved his nineties movies?

I also became genuinely good at a few things. Bread, soups, pasta from scratch. Anything that required time and patience, in an environment where the attention span hovers between Agitated Toddler and Agitated Wasp.

An example: The following summer, we put a tomato consommé on the menu.

Diced cucumber; vacuum-packed watermelon cubes, sliced and fanned; a thin splash of olive oil. The garnishes were placed in the cold bowl, the consommé poured tableside. Simplicity itself.

Right?

Wrong. The consommé had to be perfectly clear, or you couldn't see the *garni*. The French say that if you drop a coin to the bottom of a consommé, you should be able to tell the year it was minted.

For obvious sanitary reasons, you shouldn't do this.

But you get the idea.

To make the consommé, you simply blend delicious tomatoes with garlic, salt, and a little pepper, then let the mixture strain through cheesecloth and a chinois. When the other cooks made it, it turned out cloudy. When I did it, it turned out clear. The trick was to make it first thing in the morning, and let gravity push the clear liquid through. If you made it just before service, and tried to push the

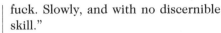

"I mean, Christ—what the hell am I going to tell the wife?"

liquid through with a ladle—something you can do with other kinds of soup—all the little impurities came through, and ruined it.

One Sunday morning in July, Brett Anderson, the restaurant critic for the *Times-Picayune*, came in for brunch. New Orleans doesn't have the Michelin Guide, or a star system like *The New York Times*. Anderson was here because he was preparing his Top 10 guide for the fall.

Of course, he ordered the consommé. A Sunday morning in New Orleans, and instead of our chicken and waffles, eggs benedict, or shrimp and grits, he ordered tomato fucking consommé.

It was an outrage. Like going to a Texas roadhouse and ordering vichyssoise.

The chef asked for the quart container with that morning's consommé, and a spoon. It was too late to make another batch. Unlike pretty much everything else on the menu, it was impossible to remake on the fly.

Until this point, I had been feeling a bit like Gomer Pyle, when it turns out he's actually a good marksman. But now, like Pyle, I realized I had become a little too attached. And you know how that one ended.

What's important to remember here is that consommé is really just flavored water. Savory La Croix. Not really food at all.

Nevertheless, I plated. Dice of cucumbers. Fan of watermelon. Dash of oil. Chef poured the consommé in the carafe, then we waited in the kitchen as Jacob, our star waiter, delivered it to the table.

Surely, even on the off-chance he liked the dish, Anderson wouldn't actually say anything, right? Aren't all food writers jaded hedonists, continually fussed over and forever unsatisfied? If he hated it, would he actually go so far as to tell the server?

And didn't he know that I was surrounded by a platoon of bloodthirsty Marines, bars of soap and towels at the ready?

Jacob came back a few minutes later, nearly out of breath. "Brett said he liked it so much, he wished he could give a spoonful to every diner in the restaurant." I thought I heard clapping, but that was my imagination.

What I really heard was the sound of a half-dozen bludgeons, being dropped to the floor all at once. Followed by the genuine sighs of a kitchen full of disappointed sadists.

"Tebow, you did that!" chef exclaimed. By which he meant, of all people.

Still, I felt a great sense of pride when we made the Top 10 that year. Even better, Anderson actually feted the consommé in his capsule review.

I stayed on for another year, and worked my way up the line. But to the rest of the kitchen, I knew I would always be Gomer Pyle. I mean Kyle. I mean Tebow.

Or, as Joker put it:

"Is that you, John Wayne? Is this me?" **B**

Australian Matthew Thompson designs for animation. Currently he works in the community and lives with his pet brother.

Elvis is Alive and Well

Seymour Chwast
Steven Brower

inside these pages

Contents

www.yoebooks.com

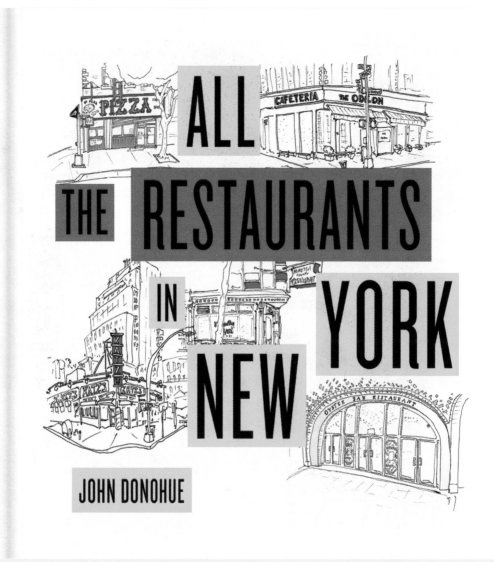

NOTES FROM A SMALL PLANET

The love that dare not meow its name • By Rick Geary

I MARRIED A CAT — RICK GEARY ©20

ONE DAY SHE JUST SHOWED UP AT MY DOOR.

HER ANTICS WOULD KEEP ME AMUSED FOR HOURS ON END.

SHE WAS HAPPY TO EAT THE SAME FARE EVERY DAY.

IN TIME SHE GREW INTO A BREATHTAKING CREATURE.

SHE COULD BE FIERCELY LOYAL AND PROTECTIVE.

IN FACT, SHE RIPPED TO SHREDS ANY FEMALE WHO CAME NEAR ME.

WHAT COULD I DO BUT MARRY HER?

OUR FAMILIES AND FRIENDS BITTERLY DIVIDED.

THO AT FIRST WE WERE QUITE HAPPY, CERTAIN DIFFICULTIES SOON AROSE.

SHE INSISTED UPON STAYING OUT ALL NIGHT...

AND BROUGHT HOME THE MANGLED CARCASSES OF SMALL ANIMALS.

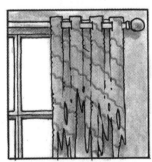
EPISODES OF DESTRUCTIVE BEHAVIOR SHE WOULD DISMISS AS NO BIG DEAL.

WE SPENT MANY HOURS IN THERAPY.

TOO MANY COUPLES SPLIT UP THESE DAYS OVER MINOR DISAGREEMENTS.

OUR FIRST LITTER IS ON THE WAY!

B

visit
www.rosenworld.com

for
**Sneakers, Signed Books,
Melty Jewels
and Original Artwork**
by **Laurie Rosenwald**, First Pancake,
Occasional Swede
**& America's
Favorite Bystander**

**"Laurie's voice is fresh sounding,
funny, and completely her own." -David Sedaris**

WHAT AM I DOING HERE?

The sign over Lenin's Tomb read, "DO NOT MAKE JOKES." So, naturally... • By Mike Reiss

IN FRONT OF LENIN'S TOMB: *Your author, moments before a minor, entirely predictable international incident.*

From Russia With Like

23 and Me told me I was 98.7% Jewish, and I thought, "Really, that little?" And when you're Jewish, you don't care about revisiting your roots. Because this isn't the country you came from, it's the country you were chased out of. In my case, I'm half Russian, and my family's story is so sad it makes *Fiddler on the Roof* look like a musical. I mean, *Fiddler on the Roof* is already a musical, but I was referring to a happy musical like *Annie* not a sad one like, uh, *Fiddler on the Roof.*

Nonetheless, I've visited Russia twice: the first time, with a tour group in 2001. The country was not quite ready for us. Every couple of hours our tour bus would stop in the woods and our guide would tell us, "This is your toilet stop. This is truly a wonderful forest to urinate in." It was summer, the temperatures hovered around 100 degrees, and the hotels had no air conditioning. Each night, you could sleep with the windows open and be eaten alive by mosquitoes, or close the windows and be baked alive.

MIKE REISS is Intrepid Traveler for *The American Bystander*.

Those were your options: freedom of choice had come to Russia. Crime had come too—there was no restaurant, bar or hotel in any corner of the world's largest country, that was not being shaken down by the Russian mob.

The tour group I was traveling with was largely elderly and largely never shut up. But their endless chattering stopped abruptly when we entered Red Square and laid eyes on The Kremlin. My fellow tourists were children of the Cold War, and this building represented pure evil and the threat of nuclear annihilation. Now the red brick building with the candy-colored domes seemed cute and small and toothless— just like them.

For the record, the Kremlin is the fortified wall around Red Square. What everyone calls "the Kremlin" is actually St. Basil's Cathedral, which would never be the seat of power for the atheistic Communist regime. It's like confusing the White House with the Waffle House, which was true only during the Clinton Administration.

Not far from what everyone calls "the Kremlin" is Lenin's Tomb, a structure no bigger than a newsstand.

You descend a short flight of steps to visit the waxy figure that may be Lenin, but is probably a wax figure. There are large signs in several languages reading "DO NOT MAKE JOKES."

So, of course, I made a joke. I asked, "Do they dress Lenin in different outfits for the holidays?" My wife laughed and a guard pointed a machine gun at her.

Interestingly, the Russians want to get rid of Lenin's Tomb—it honors a man who brought their country a repressive regime that collapsed after seventy years. It's only open to make the tourists happy, as I'm sure Trump's Tomb someday will be. The sooner the better, I say.

When I went back to Russia two decades later, everything had changed. The Cold War was over and Western decadence had won. Moscow's Tverskaya Street rivaled New York's Fifth Avenue for high-end shopping and fine dining. Good food in Russia? *That's* a revolution! It was a warm Russian winter, with temperatures in the high nothings, and this once-godless country had gone cuckoo for Christmas. Red Square went over the top with lights and decorations; wherever there wasn't real snow, there was fake snow. Lenin's Tomb was flush up against Santa's Workshop.

In true capitalist spirit, I was in Russia on business: I'd been asked to

Explore the world's largest cartoon database

ZEITGEIST

YOU ARE HERE
★

give a lecture on *The Simpsons* to an audience of ex-Soviet entrepreneurs. Whenever I get an offer like this, my first question is always, "Who did you ask first?" In this case, it was Uma Thurman. Of course. If you can't get the gorgeous, world-famous actress, bring in some Jew you never heard of. But the weird surprise was they *had* heard of me—the Russians, for some reason, go absolutely *bolshoi* for *The Simpsons*! When my limo arrived at the hotel—yes, they sent a limo!—I was mobbed by paparazzi. Autograph hounds waved publicity photos of me that I didn't even know existed. My hotel, by the way, was the Moscow Ritz, where Donald Trump allegedly romped and, let's say, "showered" with four prostitutes. Having stayed there, I believe it—my suite was so luxurious, you'd feel like you could get away with anything. And the décor was so baroque, the KGB could hide cameras anywhere.

I arrived at the venue the next morning—it was Moscow Olympic Stadium, and I'd be addressing fifteen thousand Russian entrepreneurs. That's a lot of entrepreneurs for a former Communist dictatorship. Many in the audience spoke English—the rest received simultaneous translation through headphones. The opening speaker was announced: Richard Gere! He strolled onstage to dead silence. He flashed his dazzling movie star grin and proclaimed, "Hello Moscow! I love this city!"

More dead silence. None of the speakers who followed him got much response either—not Malcolm Gladwell, not the Ultimate Fighting Champion of the World. We were a pretty random assortment of speakers—the only thing we had in common was that nobody wanted to listen to us. It was seven hours of thunderous indifference, broken up by a lunch where the businessmen downed liquor like Prohibition was coming back. I was the final speaker, and, as BBC Russia reported, "Tonight, Mike Reiss told great jokes to a gravely silent audience."

I shrugged it off—I figured this was how Russian audiences always were. I asked the Russian organizer how she thought the day went.

She said, "This was a complete disaster. Tomorrow, they are tearing down the stadium."

That's a pretty harsh review—*you were so bad, they tore down the venue.* Still, I felt proud. My ancestors left this country a century ago without a penny in their pockets. I was leaving with a speaker's fee of ten thousand dollars.

When I got home, the check bounced. It bounced and bounced and may still be bouncing. I've lectured on *The Simpsons* in twenty-two countries and that's the only time that happened. You can read about it in my *Simpsons* memoir *Springfield Confidential*. It's available in English, Spanish, German, and we recently sold the Russian-language rights.

That check bounced too.   ◼

ROZ'S MARVELOUS COLLAGES

Japanese matchbox covers from anonymous artists, 1920-1940 • By Roz Chast

P.S. MUELLER THINKS LIKE THIS

The cartoonist/broadcaster/writer is always walking around, looking at stuff • By P.S. Mueller

Civilization

Archeologists made an earthshaking discovery while excavating a site in Egypt's Valley of Kings: a perfectly preserved iPhone in the tomb of Phil Johnson.

It was still charging.

He had become the founder of the Johnson Dynasty, as a sun god and pretty good gin rummy player. Phil wore a business suit and tie and said a lot of things like, "Thank you for reaching out" and "Let me be clear."

Everyone in the kingdom started dressing for business. They came and went to Phil's court. (He preferred to be called "Phil," and he liked forms.)

And the valley prospered under Phil's rule, especially after his armies drove off the Elephant People. I think the E.P. moved to Montecito, California, and opened banks. They sort of mixed in and moved along anyway. I don't know.

Back to Phil: the ancient iPhone was a tantalizing discovery, but there was a problem: the pass code was unavailable.

The world's foremost engineers gathered in Bettendorf, Iowa, where they parsed code for nearly a century until they finally dug up Steve Jobs and discovered the passcode tattooed behind his left ear.

The phone, registered to Phil Johnson,

P.S. MUELLER is Staff Liar of *The American Bystander*.

revealed unknown histories of rulers, wars, proxy battles, copyright disputes, and nasty jokes about Jeff Bezos. It was all petty stuff and—like old COBOL or DOS—it was layered and redundant, kind of mixed in with what we have today, though. However, the device also contained the lost history of continents long gone, and the early comedies of Sordo were there, too. Though it turned out they were all shot as *Honeymooners* episodes in the 1950s.

Peckerwood Hts.

Life stumbled on in Peckerwood Heights. Fading cheerleaders, fierce and determined, walked stern dogs through red mud in L.L. Bean boots.

L.L. Bean was exhausted and most of the workers were dead anyway. Nevertheless, Peckerwood carried on. I stood on my back porch which was double-wrapped in filter mesh. Quality filter mesh! Virus-proof.

Along came a lady who was selling little things made out of yarn: God's eyes, dream-catchers, and what have you. She was fifty and thick with dreadlocks. "It'll cure the huckles," she brayed.

The huckles were indeed a problem. By then variants were loose upon the world. A mild case offered no symptoms. A bad case involved what was called "The shrieking gurgle." The onset began with a slight clearing of the throat, soon followed by a violent torrent of nausea. Streets, sidewalks, lawns, and parks were to be avoided. Usually, victims died quickly and had to be buried before the next moon-down. The idea was to cover them with soil and just sort of tamp tamp

tamp away until the muffled screaming faded and stopped. Fortunately, they liquified quickly. Texas congressman Louie Gohmert succumbed. and was dumpstered and thoroughly hosed from the spot.

Some time ago. Tony Fauci suggested split pea soup during a hot mic moment. It might cure anything, he said.

The Roads

I remember the old days when folks drove on the roads. It was OK.

But it was too costly to repair the roads anymore. And besides, roads had melted into the ground and became hard to find. There were "road islands" too, places with remnants where people could still drive—for a little ways. But you couldn't drive to them.

Then old man Pemberton got himself flattened where 224 used to be. He just stuck there like a North Dakota pheasant. He didn't even flap in the wind. Not old man Pemberton. He just sort of dried out and quivered, mail scattered around him; that flapped a little.

One piece was an AT&T bill from 1992. It was overdue. Pemberton knew none of this because he was flat. Neighbor kids peeled him up and scrolled him. Then they threw him away.

But you should have seen these roads when they were sinking—asphalt and gravel going this way and that. Why did it happen? It turned out that the center of the Earth was full of plastic bags, and it wanted some REAL MATTER. That's when the roads and freeways and bridges began to sink. **B**

CLASSIFIEDS

Lucas Adams

FLASH SALE! 40% OFF!
New editions of out-of-print comic/cartooning masterpieces and new translations of books that have never been published in English. Check it out: www.nyrb.com/collections/new-york-review-comics

INSTAGRAM: @ lucaswadams
www.lucaswilliamadams.com

Jeff Albers

The Onion once called me "the single worst part of humanity."
MEDIUM: jeffalbers.medium.com
TWITTER: @jeffralbers
www.jeffalbers.com

Jaylee Alde

COWABUNGA
An attempt at parody, a push towards satire, but history will call it non-fiction.
Available now at **amazon.com**

TWITTER: @jayleealde

Luke Atkinson

On Instagram at
@lukealexatkinson
More drawings & updates at
365cdn.tumblr.com

Ikenna Azuike

PRESENTER, FILMMAKER, WRITER,
actor, producer, cashew fan.
Credits: **What's Up Africa**
(BBC), Planet Nigeria (BNN VARA), The Post-Racist Planet (VPRO Tegenlicht). Find me on Twitter: **@IkennaAzuike**.
jollofriceproductions.com

Ian Baker

THE CODGERS' Kama Sutra
Everything you always wanted to know about sex, but were too tired to ask!
IAN BAKER

THE CODGERS' KAMA SUTRA
Available at **Amazon.co.uk**.

www.ianbakercartoons.co.uk
TWITTER: @IanCartoonist

Melissa Balmain

L I G H T

Losing your mind? Try LIGHT.
America's premier magazine of funny poetry since 1992
Edited by Melissa Balmain
lightpoetrymagazine.com
TWITTER:
@LightPoetryMagazine
FACEBOOK:
LightPoetryMagazine

Jeremy Banks

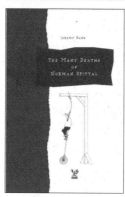

JEREMY BANKS
THE MANY DEATHS OF NORMAN SPITTAL

Signed copies of
THE MANY DEATHS OF NORMAN SPITTAL
Available at **Amazon.co.uk**.

www.banxcartoons.co.uk
TWITTER: @banxcartoons
FACEBOOK: jeremy.banks.391

Ron Barrett

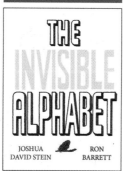
THE INVISIBLE ALPHABET
JOSHUA DAVID STEIN   RON BARRETT

THE INVISIBLE ALPHABET
An ABC of Things Unseen: from Air to Zero, and Nothing In Between.
Written by **Joshua David Stein**. Illustrated by **Ron Barrett**.
"Make sure to see this A+ alphabet book"
–A Kirkus Starred Review.
Available at **Amazon**.

Mark Bazer

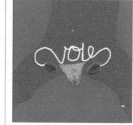
The Interview Show

THE INTERVIEW SHOW
is a talk show in a bar...on TV. Taped at The Hideout, a legendary dive bar in Chicago, each episode features two or three conversations that are as substantive as they are entertaining, along with short comedic sketches.
https://interactive.wttw.com/interview-show

Lou Beach

"Funny, smart, twisted, brilliant...**the greatest collage artist on the planet**..." –TERRY GILLIAM, *film director*

Stories and pictures at
loubeach.com

Tracey Berglund

Portraits & Illustration

Kamala Harris

INSTAGRAM: @tra4art
FACEBOOK: tracey.berglund

Louisa Bertman

Editorial illustrator
gif guru
animator & filmmaker
www.louisabertman.com
INSTAGRAM: @louisabertman
FACEBOOK: louisabertman
TWITTER: @louisabertman

Michael Ian Black

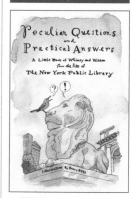
"Raw, intimate, and true."
—PEGGY ORENSTEIN, bestselling author of *Boys & Sex*
A BETTER MAN
A (Mostly Serious) Letter to My Son
Michael Ian Black

A BETTER MAN:
A (MOSTLY SERIOUS) LETTER TO MY SON
"Raw, intimate, and true . . . *A Better Man* cracked me wide open, and it's a template for the conversation we need to be having with our boys."
–**Peggy Orenstein**
Available at **Powell's**.

TWITTER: @michaelianblack
www.michaelianblack.com

R.O. Blechman

SIGNED PRINTS, BOOKS & more
www.roblechman.com
See our ad on p. 56!

PHOTO: LEE FRIEDLANDER

Harry Bliss

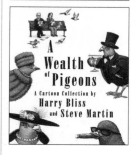
A Wealth of Pigeons
A Cartoon Collection by Harry Bliss and Steve Martin

A WEALTH OF PIGEONS
Cartoons created by Bystander Harry Bliss and legendary standup Steve Martin. "Surreal, silly, satirical and, at times, oddly moving."
–The Washington Post
Available at **Powell's**.

INSTAGRAM: @blisscartoons

Barry Blitt

Peculiar Questions and Practical Answers
A Little Book of Whimsy and Wisdom from the Files of The New York Public Library
Illustration by Barry Blitt

PECULIAR QUESTIONS AND PRACTICAL ANSWERS
A Little Book of Whimsy and Wisdom from the Files of The New York Public Library.
Illustrated by Barry Blitt
Available at **Amazon**.

www.barryblitt.com

Roy Blount, Jr.

Save Room for Pie
FOOD SONGS AND CHEWY RUMINATIONS
ROY BLOUNT JR.

SAVE ROOM FOR PIE
Food Songs and Chewy Ruminations
"Blount is the best. He can be literate, uncouth and soulful all in one sentence."
–Garrison Keillor, writing in
The Paris Review
Available at **Amazon**.

www.royblountjr.com

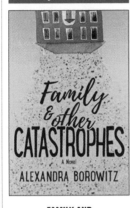

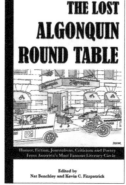

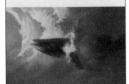

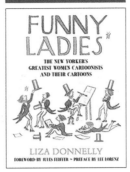

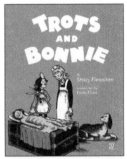

THE
NEW NORMAL